GW00499450

THRIVE NOW
Blueprint

Self-Care & Success Strategies for
Parents of Special Needs Children

Siobhán Wilcox

Thrive Now Blueprint Self-Care and Success Strategies for Parents of Special Needs Children

Text Copyright © 2014 by Siobhan Wilcox
Cover design and Interior layout: Cory Wright
Backcover and Interior photographs: Monique Feil
Editing: Anne Marie Welsh

First Edition

Last Reviewed June 2014

ISBN: 978-0-9905766-0-0

Published by The Wilcox-Ward Group Inc.

For feedback, inquiries related to the book, or for consulting, speaking, interviews and training inquires, email Siobhan@SiobhanWilcox.com

For more information and for upcoming Thrive Now events and trainings visit www.SiobhanWilcox.com

Printed in the United States of America
Keywords: Parenting, Parenting Special Needs, Self-Care, Stress Management, Self-help, Transformation, Personal Development.

For Oisin, Aran and Paul
my greatest teachers and the
unwinged angels in my world

To all the beautiful animals that are part of our family
& especially in loving memory of Howard the Hero!

To my Mam & Dad
who always believed in me and encouraged me to soar

Praise for
Thrive Now Blueprint

"Finally - a book I can recommend to parents about the most important aspect of raising a special needs child – self-care! Kudos to Siobhan Wilcox for writing the book that we need to stay healthy and serene in the midst of all that being a parent of a special needs child entails.
Flight attendants tell you that in case of an emergency, you must take care of yourself before attending to your children. The same is true in real life. Thrive Now Blueprint is a practical guide with strategies that are doable for parents who are time, energy and money- constrained. In Thrive Now Blueprint, Siobhan guides parents through short exercises that help parents create healthy self care habits that only take a few minutes at a time. Siobhan has taken her 16 years of experience as a Stress Management Expert and applied them to her needs as the mother of a child on the autism spectrum. I highly recommend this book for all parents of special needs children and those in the helping professions"
Chantal Sicile-Kira, Founder of AutismCollege.com; author of five books including: *Autism Spectrum Disorder (revised): The Complete Guide to Understanding Autism.*

"As Siobhan Wilcox knows, parenting a child with additional needs is both a beautiful and a challenging experience. In the Thrive Now Blueprint she offers up wisdom from her professional and personal life to help parents find greater balance, relieve stress and live healthier lives. I would recommend the book to any parent in need of techniques for greater health and happiness, for the benefit of themselves and their families."
Torrie Dunlap, CEO, Kids Included Together, non–profit organization serving as a center for the understanding and practice of inclusion.

"Practicing self care is the greatest lesson I can model for our son and one of the most important gifts I can give him. The more I thrive and give to him from my overflow, the better parent I will be for him. Siobhan Wilcox's book, Thrive Now Blueprint, guides parents down this road with compassion and valuable insights. An empowering and important read for all special needs parents."
Kalli Holmes Sorensen, Mother of a son on the autism spectrum and the Founder of the Seaside Sisters- A Women's Empowerment Ministry

Praise from past clients for
Siobhan Wilcox

"Siobhan is an amazing coach, and I feel very graced to have had the opportunity to work with her. Siobhan has had challenges in her life, and is, therefore, not only able to really understand and empathize with her clients, but she is able to use her life experience to help others in a very real way. Siobhan has an uncanny ability to guide you through your own challenges and blocks in a very supportive and empowering way. She is a very strong leader, yet offers her guidance in very loving and effective ways. She leads by example, and demonstrates the highest integrity and warmth. I highly recommend working with her! You won't be disappointed"

Nancy G – Founder, CEO at Xolos For Chronic Pain Relief X-CPR

"Siobhan is amazing. My life changed for the better immediately after seeing her and it was so enriching! Everything just fell into place. I recommend her highly." –

Kathy R – Company Director and busy single mom

"We've been painting, dancing and having lots of family fun! Thank you for your love and guidance."

Parents of Special Needs Child, San Diego

"I have taken two workshops from Siobhan, and have really benefited from her guidance in setting goals and finding more joy in my life. Her caring attitude is genuine, and it has helped me to live my life more in tune with my inner light."

Chris M, San Diego

"I wanted to thank you again for the workshop. I'd hoped to get spiritual renewal from it and I did that. I got back in touch with things I have learned on my spiritual journey and learned some new things. Most important, you reminded me that I need to pay attention to my thoughts. Thank you so much for your wisdom and insight. You are a shining light."

Lorraine I, San Diego

Acknowledgments

To my husband Paul Ward who supported me while I wrote this book, making me lunches, reading my musings, doing the school pick ups if needed to give me space. I love you.

To my mother – Mary Wilcox who supported me with her incredible editing skills, belief in my project and her ability to keep my grammar in check, thanks so much- love you mom. To my dad, John Wilcox who always believed in me and taught me the gifts of spending time in nature and in quiet reflection. Love you dad.

To my brilliant editor Anne Marie Welsh who encouraged me to keep going when I hit my writer's wall and helped me craft this book. You are a brilliant 'Book Doctor'.

To my stress management mentors Mary Scarff and Michael Hughes. Thank you for guiding me to heal my own body, mind and spirit and then encouraging me to chose this as a career. Your belief in me was the catalyst I needed to see my own potential as someone who could serve others in the same way you gave me support.

To my beautiful loving boys Aran & Oisin. Thank you so much for choosing to be on this journey with me – I love you deeply and honor you always.

To all the beautiful parents who shared their stories with me. Thank you for your insights. You supported the unfolding of this book. I hope it meets your needs.

To all my friends who put up with my rantings over the last couple of years as this project developed. Thanks for never telling me to be quiet. Thanks for being my cheerleaders and for telling me to keep on!

Thanks to all my clients who allowed me to support them with my gifts over the last 16 years and consistently verified that I was on the right path.
A big thank you to all the 'beautiful souls' we have met along our path of parenting – those who have seen the gifts in our sons and helped them shine, those who have advocated for us, particularly Nancy Lazerson who has been our guiding angel on more then one occasion.

To all my family who supported with loving comments and energy as you are all wonderful.

Table of Content

Introduction

"And in the end it's not the years in your life that count; it's the life in your years."

Abraham Lincoln (1809-1865); 16th US President

Our Collective Power

*T*his book is a gathering of heart-centered wisdoms for parents of special needs children, offered by myself and other parents who are also on this journey. When I discovered my child was on the autism spectrum, I felt as though I had been thrown overboard without a life jacket. I felt alone, isolated, and I was plunged into grief. Yet life went on around me and I have not only managed to survive, I am thriving. Along the way, I have encountered incredible parents who are thriving, laughing, sharing and inspiring others. Just as the Native American Indians gathered stories to share their wisdom and spiritual beliefs among their tribe, so I feel compelled to do the same by sharing my years of wisdom alongside tales from others living this life too. Tales filled with compassion, insights, self-care, transformation and miracles. This work is not about how to cure your child; it is about thriving, regardless of how your child is. However, I have discovered that the more I nurture myself, the calmer my child is.

Thrive Now Blueprint is designed for parents of special needs children to help them create a self-care plan, learn simple ways to deeply relax, increase their vitality levels, reduce their stress levels and live a more self-nurturing life. Everyone can use the tools and techniques I outline to help gain significant balance in their lives.

I am passionate about helping parents of children on the autism spectrum because as a mother of a boy on the spectrum, I have unique insights that many outside that circle do not have. I am also a stress management consultant, spiritual life coach and intuitive with more than twenty years' experience.

When I was a child I thought I would become a nun. I had such a deep connection with God, but then I fell in love with my first boyfriend and that was the end of any thought of entering the convent! However I had a knowing from around six that I could heal the pain of others. I have memories of inviting family members and friends who were in physical pain to sit so I could support them. My best friend at the time remembered me massaging her when I was eight. Everyone thought it was cute, however, years later I still had the same desire to support those in pain. By the age of twenty, I began training in counseling skills, then went on to study massage therapy and other modalities to support the creation of balance – mind, body and spirit. By the age of twenty-nine, I was working with business leaders as a personal development trainer and stress management consultant and teaching spiritual practices at the weekends.

As a child, I spent many hours in church talking to Jesus and God. Now as an adult, I spend many hours supporting those searching for a deeper spiritual connection, increased inner peace and more balance. In the past I've worked with the long-term unemployed, special needs care-workers, single moms with challenging children, business leaders in need of guidance, burning-out executives, to name but a few. However I feel it was all building to now, my true passion path, supporting a community that I understand intimately, my sisters and brothers in arms. Those living a life that is often challenging yet under-resourced and over-stressed on a daily basis.

How to get the best from this book

*E*ach chapter contains a core concept for increasing well-being. I include a number of reflective exercises with journaling space for you to record your feelings and insights. At the end of each chapter is an area for goal setting. Don't feel that you must make big, ambitious goals. I have found that when I made small commitments that were possible to achieve, instead of trying to change everything all at the same time, real change and transformation happened for me. Make sure you date your goals so you can look back and see how far you've come along your Thrive pathway.

I suggest you make a weekly or monthly goal or commitment to yourself. Make these short and manageable so that they are achievable. It will increase your success and help anchor in the new learning.

Although I have a lot of experience helping myself and others stay balanced, I realized that I only had my own viewpoint, so I decided to gather wisdom from other special parents to share their inspirations. I had the great honor to interview some amazing Moms who had a wealth of insights.

These **'Wisdoms from the Front Line'** are contained in Chapter 13. This chapter contains three interviews with amazing 'super' moms just like you. More interviews and wisdoms are featured at my online resource, which is available EXCLUSIVELY for readers of this book. Details on registering to access this powerful Thrive Now ToolKit are on page 16.

Just expressing your goals and commitments in a supportive community helps to anchor them in place and makes them more attainable. To help with this ongoing motivation and support I have created a **Thrive Now Blueprint Facebook Community** where you can discuss your challenges and successes, or give and ask for support. Both community and mutual support are proven ways to increase results. The goal of this Facebook group is to connect you with other like-minded parents who are making **THE COMMITMENT** to make positive changes in their lives.

To support your learning I created the **Premium Online Thrive Now ToolKit** to accompany this book. As I said already this is an exclusive resource for readers of the *Thrive Now Blueprint*, and can only be accessed by those who register at www.ThriveNowToolkit.com.

Once you register – just by entering your name and email, you will be brought to a website that gives you the exercise downloads, relaxation audios, supplemental videos and bonus features. Don't worry - I will not share your emails with anyone but I will be sending you invitations to events and interviews that I think you will love to be part of!

CHAPTER 1
DREAM SHIFTING

Access the exercise sheets for this chapter
CLICK HERE NOW!

CHAPTER 2
POWER OF SELF-CARE

Access the exercise sheets for this chapter
CLICK HERE NOW!

CHAPTER 3
ONLY SUPER HEROES NEED APPLY

Access the exercise sheets for this chapter
CLICK HERE NOW!

CHAPTER 4
SABER TIGER IN THE LIVING ROOM

Access the exercise sheets for this chapter
CLICK HERE NOW!

I have created this to support you thriving. Although you do not have to signup for these I recommend that you do as they complement the work within this book and enhance your learning experience. Invite your friends and family members to get involved by reading this book too; having those around you supporting you is an enhanced recipe for THRIVING.

Just as Jannirose JOY, one of the mothers I interviewed, talks about her need to look deeply at herself with as much awareness as possible to support her family being in harmony, I invite you to participate throughout this book in the same way. This is an empowering place to be in; from here you can take action and move into thriving each day.

Visit www.SiobhanWilcox.com to buy another copy of this book and to discover my latest interview series and upcoming events. Enjoy the *Thrive Now Blueprint*!

And finally I would be honored to know the exercises you loved the most and the insights you received from completing them. You can share your inspiration on our Facebook community https://www.facebook.com/ThriveNowBlueprint or email me directly at stories@thrivenowblueprint.com

1

Dream Shifting

> **"Your living is determined not so much by what life brings to you as by the attitude you bring to life; not so much by what happens to you as by the way your mind looks at what happens."**
>
> -Khalil Gibran (1883-1931); Artist, Poet, Writer

The start of the dream

My journey of wishing to be a mother began when I was five. It was nearly Christmas and I was so excited that Santa Claus was coming. I needed to write a letter to Santa. I wrote really carefully, with my Mommy's help, to tell him exactly what I wanted. I had thought about it for months and months beforehand: I wanted my very own *Tiny Tears* baby doll. I had seen a picture of her in a toy magazine. She came with a little pink bath and a feeding bottle and she had her own baby clothes. She was just so perfect.

I remember the anticipation of that Christmas morning. I actually woke in the middle of the night, much to the frustration of my parents who shooed me back to bed, where I sat waiting for the clock to turn seven so I could finally go downstairs and meet my new baby! My body was tingling with excitement as I ripped open the wrapping paper and there she was; my very own baby doll! I held her in my arms, and then fed her. When she wet herself I could change her diaper. I felt like I was in heaven. We went everywhere together. I made a little bed for her at the end of my own bed. I was so in love with her.

Many years later, at the age of thirty-one, my son was born and my childhood dream of being a mother came true. I was beside myself with excitement at having this child. I had attended all the prenatal classes and natural birthing classes, practiced yoga each day and prenatal aqua aerobics three times a week. I did everything recommended in the pregnancy books. I ate all the right foods, including a full color range of vegetable, took my prenatal vitamins, folic acid and iron. I did it all. I really wanted to have a natural birth, so I wrote up my birth plan - no epidural, no student nurses, minimum intervention unless there was an emergency. I wanted it to be an intimate, relaxing experience.

However, my best-laid plans did not turn out as expected. My husband later described the delivery room in Dublin as similar to Grand Central Station, with staff rushing in and out, trying to assist me and also bringing babies in and out to have them checked. My labor suite turned out to be the main station for checking all the babies' vital signs, yet I was oblivious to all this commotion. All I knew was that this baby needed to come out and come out soon, because I had been in labor, on and off, for three days. But every time he tried to come out, for some reason he kept getting stopped and his heart rate would drop. Then he went into distress. The medical team was worried and suggested an emergency C-section, yet we never got that far. Suddenly I heard a shout from the nurse: "Stop pushing, the cord is around his neck!"

I was gripped with fear and knowledge at the same time. Because we had been in labor together for so long, I already knew something was wrong. Adeptly the nurse unwrapped the umbilical cord and finally, after our marathon together, my beautiful baby was born. The cord had seemingly done "no damage", according to the staff on duty.

I remember the nurse placing him in my arms. I looked deeply at him. I felt as if my heart had burst open; his energy was like fluffy pink clouds. I was awash with love, joy and relief. In that moment, I made a promise to him, right there and then: "I will always love you and I will always protect you, and I will do whatever it takes for you to have a magnificent life".

We named him Oisin, meaning "little fawn" in Gaelic. Oisin also holds high stature in Irish Myth as the greatest poet that Ireland ever had, the son of the great Irish warrior Fionn mac Cumhaill. Little did I realize that I would need to embody much warrior energy to support my son in the commitment I had made to him. At the time, Oisin seemed a fitting name for this new soul that had been entrusted to us. Our beloved son seemed so gentle and soft in nature and I started calling him my baby angel.

Even within the first few hours, it was noticeable that there was something a little different about my son. He could not latch on to breast-feed.

Although I had taken courses in breast-feeding and in natural feeding workshops and although the nurses worked with me for hours, we just could not make it happen. Oisin could not get his mouth to latch, he could not figure out how to suck. He was so distressed and obviously hungry. The nurses suggested I try a bottle. So much to my despair, I resorted to bottle-feeding him.

He was a beautiful, gentle baby but he cried and cried. He liked to be wrapped tightly and he wanted to be held all the time. He never needed to nap during the day. For this to happen, I had to drive him around in my car, and hope that he would fall asleep. When he did, I would pull over to the side of the road, release my seat back and recline, thinking "Ooohhh, rest time for me!" Sometimes I would nap in the driveway because, if I moved him, he would instantly wake up and our rest would be over for the day.

At six weeks, he had an allergic reaction to his first vaccine. At eight weeks, he had surgery to repair the groin hernia that the reaction created. His intestines had swollen to create two hernias: one where his belly button grew to the size of a lime, and the second that looked like a third testicle.

Looking for solutions

His reaction to the vaccine launched my journey to find holistic therapists who could work with my ultra-sensitive boy. I explored the fields of *Touch for Health* kinesiology, cranial sacral therapy, color and aura soma therapy. These all seemed to help him maintain balance and experience less pain. I made all his baby food, steamed, puréed, and blended organic food each week and stored it in ice-cube trays. Although life became easier for me as I learned how to manage him, it became obvious that my son's ability to speak and use language was not developing normally. We arranged speech therapy for severe speech delay and when he was four years of age, doctors diagnosed him with both speech and motor apraxia. However, when he started preschool, new difficulties began to present.

In preschool, he needed to be able to follow directions and accept structure in a group environment. This was difficult for him. I would regularly get phone calls from preschool: "He's overwhelmed again and we're not sure what triggered it." In time, it became apparent that moving from one activity to another was a trigger-point; 'transitioning' was a major difficulty. Everyday situations such as managing the transition between the playground and the classroom were too much for him. Similarly, the transition to stop what he was doing and go sit with the Reverend to listen to a bible story was too much for him.

This insight led to another stage of my journey; as a parent I had to consistently help regulate my son's behavior. Initially, friends and family members reassured my husband and me that his constant overwhelming happened because he was shy and not able to communicate. However, by the age of seven the overwhelming had not stopped although by now his speech was very clear. Eventually, he was diagnosed as being on the autistic spectrum, high functioning.

One dream dies

In the moment of getting that diagnosis my world stopped. I fell apart completely. I thought to myself, this is not the plan. The plan that I had made at the age of five, the plan that I had created all the way through my life up until that moment, the plan of going on exotic family vacations and attending community events, watching my son perhaps graduate from college, being the doting mother of the groom. This diagnosis was not part of my plan.

I had worked as a stress management consultant and a personal development instructor for fifteen years. In that time I had helped thousands of people on their journeys through life. I helped them find balance, helped them find peace through meditation, helped them develop self-care skills in the areas of nutrition and diet, helped them create joy in their lives and love for their true selves.

Now here I was, the teacher, the person whom people came to when they had a problem, the one clients called when they had life challenges—and here I was: I could not stop crying. I cried and cried and cried. I spent days crying. I was just about able to pull it together when school time was finished, just about able to go through the basic functioning of getting food to the table, getting laundry done, answering some emails from my clients in an almost numbed way, and then crying again. I didn't understand why I was crying. I couldn't put it together. I couldn't figure out the pieces; all I knew was that the tears just wouldn't stop.

Then a very dear and wise friend said to me, "You're grieving". I said, "Okay, if it's grief, why? What am I grieving for?" Then, like a lightning bolt, it hit me – I was grieving for the dream that had begun when I was a little, red-haired five year old girl. That dream was shattered - the idyllic scenes of motherhood that had been with me since I was a child were not possible. Surprisingly, this realization gave me an anchor to work with.

Making a new plan

I knew I needed to create a new dream with new goals and expectations. I remembered the promise that I had made to my son when he was born, "I will do anything to make sure you have a magnificent life". I started to reexamine my thoughts and feelings. What was it that I truly wanted for my son, my family and myself?

It seemed that I wanted for him what I had had. Eventually I came to accept that maybe that wasn't his journey. Maybe his path was different and unique. I had tried to put upon him my "perfect" plan: go to college, get a job; find what in your life he was most passionate about and turn that into a career that supports him; find someone to spend the rest of his life with, get married, have children, have grandchildren.

My plan! I realized that this plan did not necessarily need to be my son's plan. His journey was his own, and he would have unique gifts to share with the world as well as a unique way of looking at the world. Despite his issues, he was highly intelligent, gifted with technology, funny, loving, creative and sensitive.

Of course, schooling is such an overwhelming focus in our children's early years that it was hard for me to adjust that particular dream, but I have managed to do that. I'm not saying that my son cannot get 'A's in his studies, but how and what he achieves academically is no longer my primary focus. Nurturing him to have a fulfilled life that is aligned with his uniqueness what I sometimes call 'divine mission' and the gifts that he is here to share with the world is now my intention. This is quite different to running *my* agenda for him.

When the pain that had seared through me with the shattering of my dream lifted, I had more space in my mind to create an alternative dream; slowly, the distress I had felt because of the gap between my picture and the reality dissipated. My stress reduced and my perceptions shifted so I could start dreaming again. Since this realization I have supported many people in unfolding their own **divine missions** or **true passion paths**.

As I went through my own fear of letting go perceived expectations of what 'should' be and started to allow what 'could' be, much of my pain released.

Although the dream had shifted, it was just as special, yet different. I still believed in my son's ability to be magnificent and to live a magnificent life. I still had other important pieces from my original plan, pieces like love, harmony, balance, and co-creative energy with my family. I valued and focused on these aspects of the original plan. That's what I wanted. The other stuff— the degree from MIT, the masters, or the doctorate, the wedding, the grandchildren— they were just markers of what I thought success meant.

I remembered the famous quote from the great sprinter, Wilma Rudolph: "The doctors told me I would never walk; my mother told me I would. I believed my mother". Wilma had been a sickly, crippled child who went on to break world records for running and who took three gold medals in the 1960 Olympics. She had been diagnosed with polio but her mother would not give up on her; she was determined to give her the life she deserved. Wilma was the twentieth of twenty-two children in her family, so, as you can imagine, there was little money for care and no transportation. Her mother had to carry her to the bus station that would bring them forty miles to the nearest hospital that accepted black patients.

I believe in miracles! I have spoken to many amazing parents whose children were labeled as unteachable or unreachable and yet these children went on to become authors, poets and scholars. In particular, Lyrica Mia stands out. As a child, Lyrica was unable to communicate with those around her. She seemed trapped in her autistic world. Now Lyrica Mia is an author and spiritual teacher. Using assisted technology, she amazes others with her insights and wisdom. Equally special is Charlie Fenimore who has not let his Down syndrome stop him from achieving brilliance. He calls himself an Earth Angel, writes poetry and was recently ordained a spiritual peacemaker by author and musician, James Twyman.

Taking care of yourself

Developing awareness around my dream was such a gift. It reduced the emotional triggers that often stimulated me into heightened stress or unnecessary overwhelm. I realized that it was my son's responsibility to create his own life plan, and not my responsibility. Yes, I was there to support him, nurture him, guide and encourage him, but not to impose my conscious or unconscious plans onto him. With this realization, I was able to take control of my emotional reactions. Eventually I could look at these emotional triggers with detachment and say: "Oh look, there goes that trigger again! I must be thinking about my old plan. Shred that plan."

It is our belief in our children and our determination as parents that helps change their lives. However this combination of belief and determination requires stamina and from my years of experience I now know that this stamina needs to be underpinned by a solid program of self-care. Otherwise it will result in burnout. So while I could create my new plan, with my goals, dreams and mission, I needed to make time to care for myself so that I had the energy to support my son along his pathway. What that path is, has yet to unfold fully. I believe that it is the life we live now and how we are in each moment that creates the future.

Later chapters in this book will provide signposts and suggestions to help you develop resilience and the emotional strength you need to lead a full and fulfilled life.

Me and my boys March 2013

In the following exercise I invite you to reflect on your own 'plan'. Uncovering it can help reduce the emotional triggers in your life, reduce your stress levels and allow you to reframe your life– dream shifting to a place that truly aligns with you and your family. When we choose to work with, for example, an occupational therapist or behavioral psychologist to support our child and help us add strategies to our daily family life that reduces sensory triggers and behavioral challenges, it also helps reduce our stress levels as parents. However when we also add the commitment to consciously support ourselves and develop a simple plan to add self-care then all the other work we have done over the years to support our child is amplified.

This exercise should help you gain personal insights and develop self-awareness, which in turn will enable you to identify emotional triggers that cause you distress.

Think about how reading this chapter has made you feel. Did it stimulate your emotions? Do you identify with the story line?

_____
_____
_____
_____
_____
_____
_____
_____

Were you aware of having a plan, or a secret dream about how your family life and your child's life would turn out? What were the key points of your plan? Maybe some pieces of this plan have really worked for you – can you identify and describe them?

_____
_____
_____
_____
_____
_____
_____

When your child's life is not progressing according to your plan, is this a cause of distress for you? Do you find that certain events or the lack of them act as trigger-points for your distress? Can you identify and describe them?

_____

_____

_____

_____

_____

_____

_____

_____

_____

What are you doing now to nurture and care for yourself so that you can be strong and supportive in helping your child to make the most of his or her abilities?

_____

_____

_____

_____

_____

_____

_____

_____

_____

> **"You are never too old to set another goal or to dream a new dream"**
> C.S. Lewis (1898 – 1963); Author

2

The Power of Self-Care

> **"Live your life from your heart. Share from your heart. And your story will touch and heal people's souls."**
> Melodie Beattie - Motivational Author

*A*s parents of special children, we usually have more responsibility than other parents. The truth is our children need us more. I was recently with a Mom whose two-year old had a temper tantrum of the usual "I want" kind. She said, "Well at least it won't last forever, right? He'll grow out of this pretty soon".

I smiled at her and shared that my beloved twelve-year-old is on the autism spectrum and unfortunately he still overwhelms regularly, a situation that could last up to two hours, and which often leaves my arms covered with bruises and bites. That is just the way it is right now. Her eyes grew large and she patted me on the back, not really knowing what to say next! But if you are a fellow special parent, you know what I mean. Often our beloved kids will still need constant care as adults and we need to be sure that we are fit, healthy, and able to keep up with them.

We Owe It To Them To Look After Ourselves!

We owe it to our children to look after ourselves, yet this can be a challenge because many of us have never been shown how to love and nurture ourselves.

Myth One:
Putting myself before others is just wrong!

Truth:
We are all 'worth it' and we deserve to make time to look after ourselves.

I grew up in Catholic Ireland, schooled by nuns. The messages I received as a child, consciously and unconsciously, were that sacrificing yourself for others was good. If you chose to martyr yourself, you would be deemed a Saint and be smiled on by God. Now what child does not want to be smiled upon by God?

However, years later when I lay on my parents' sofa exhausted and sick because I had burnt out from executive stress at the early age of 24, I realized that this message had helped create that moment. I had worked myself into the ground—sacrificing myself for someone else's business and the real sacrifice had been my own health and well-being. When I had the sense to resign as I was too sick to continue to work, the company immediately replaced me, with no special 'bonuses' for martyring myself!

Myth Two:
I can't afford to pamper myself!

Truth:
It can cost a lot in ill health and heartbreak when you don't take proper care of yourself.

This book is about life skills that will keep you healthy and help you cope. When we invest time and money in our health and well-being – mind, body and spirit, it comes back to us 10 fold as increased energy and health levels.

The tools and techniques offered here are free. Your input is your commitment and dedication to yourself. You need to **want** to be healthy for your own sake, so that when you are needed you can be fully present and available to spend time with your family. You need to ensure that you have the energy and vitality to have a life filled with opportunity and joyful living.

Myth Three:
I don't have the time to look after myself?

Truth:
You need to make the time. If you don't make the time now, you may not have the time later!

The Centers for Disease Control and Prevention estimates that 60% to 70% of all disease and illness is stress-related, so by not making the time to care for yourself you are probably reducing your years of healthy living. Now that is a heavy price to pay for self-neglect! And the true devastating price is reflected by Nancy Battye, mom of twins with cerebral palsy, in Chapter 13, where her lack of self-care resulted in her losing everything that was precious to her.

Myth Four:
You can't teach an old dog new tricks!

Truth:
Breaking old toxic habits is easier than you think.

When you continue to expand your knowledge and stretch yourself throughout your life, your brain stays more active and healthier. When my son was diagnosed with apraxia of speech at four, his therapist told me this was a neurological speech disorder. She explained that the brain and mouth muscles knew what to do, but there was a misfire in the neurons connecting them. To reprogram these neurons, she told me, he had to repeat a word correctly 40 times, and that created new pathways in the brain.

This made sense to me. Many of our world religions use forty day practices as part of their rituals and beliefs. This is not by chance, that nearly every major religion involves a forty day practice, changing a habit takes similar time. NOW DON"T PANIC! This does not require you to go live on a mountaintop for forty days and nights— although the rest might be good, right?

Honestly I fit my self-care and relaxation time in when I can such as while;

- driving
- lying in bed,
- walking my dog,
- watching television,
- on hold on the phone,
- waiting at appointments,
- standing in line at the grocery store.

To do this I use simple breathing techniques that anyone can do effectively, simple tools to relax the muscles of my body. Other powerful strategies change my internal perspective while I am in a stressful situation. You do not have to be a professional therapist or psychologist to understand or master these simple strategies; you just need to be committed to incorporate them into your daily routine and committed to choosing a life of self-care for the sake of your children.

(The best part of life is not just surviving, but thriving with passion and compassion and humor and style and generosity and kindness.))
Maya Angelou (born 1928);
Poet, Dancer, Producer, Playwright, Director, Author

Weekly Insights and Goal Setting:

Did any of these myths resonate with you? If so which ones?

_____
_____
_____
_____
_____

Between NOW and this date: ___/___/___, I choose to focus on letting of go of one myth that has held me back from self-caring for myself.
Describe:

_____
_____
_____
_____
_____
_____
_____
_____

Benefits from achieving this goal – How good will it feel?!

_____
_____
_____

Negative outcome if not achieved. Be honest with yourself.

_____
_____
_____

How I feel now that I've achieved this goal! ☺

_____
_____
_____
_____

3

Only Super Heroes Need Apply
Raising a Special Needs Child!

"Life affords no greater responsibility, no greater privilege, than the raising of the next generation."
- C. Everett Koop (1916 – 2013)
13th Surgeon General of the United States

Taking care of yourself

Our children require more from us than non-special needs kids require of their parents, and some of our children may need our care for the rest of their lives. **So, my friends, we need to be healthy!**

An unfortunate fact, which I have mentioned already (but I can't repeat often enough), is that many studies have indicated a close relationship between chronic stress and increased illness. In 2012, the biomedical reason for this was discovered and reported in a research study done at Carnegie Mellon University led by Sheldon Cohen. (Cohen 2012) In his "How stress influences disease: Study reveals inflammation as the culprit," he concludes that "inflammation plays an important role in the onset and progression of a wide range of diseases." The researchers showed the link between chronic stress and the increase of inflammation in the body, which caused those in the study to be at a higher risk of contacting a common virus used as part of the study.

Further research indicates that when autism affects families, these families show higher stress levels and risk much higher levels of divorce; some research says that divorce rates can be more than eighty percent higher than in other family units.

When I read these statistics, I was so upset that it motivated me to write this book. These statistics are not acceptable. I believe that together, as a collective, we owe it to ourselves to change these stats. We must reduce our stress levels and learn life-skills that enhance our health and sustain our relationships.

The fact is that we face a unique set of circumstances that many other parents cannot even comprehend.

Our lives are often filled with:

- Constant caring
- Daily overwhelm
- Constant demands
- Communication issues
- Restrictive need for routine
- Sensory integration problems
- Aggressive or isolating behaviors
- Increased physical demands such as lifting, carrying or sometimes restraining
- Anti-social behavior that can reduce our connection to family, friends and community

Add your own list:

-
-
-
-

We can experience:

- Lack of touch
- Sleep deprivation
- Feelings of isolation
- Lack of daily support
- Embarrassment in public places

- Higher levels of relationship stress and conflict
- Battles with school systems and government agencies
- Increased financial pressure from medical expenses and necessary therapies often not covered by our insurance policies.

Add your own list:
-
-
-
-
-

All these circumstances result in higher stress levels, exhaustion, and create our own health issues, if we do not chose to nurture ourselves.

A recent study published in March 2012 by *Penn* researchers, concluded that, on average, when a child has autism, family earnings are greatly affected; such earnings may be twenty-eight percent lower than those of a family whose child has no health limitation. Mothers fare the worst, averaging fifty-six percent less income. (Medicine 2012)

I have heard this from so many parents, parents who have compromised their careers to become stay at home care-givers. I have heard it from others whose ability to work is restricted by appointment demands and by the need to be 'on call' to assist their children daily. (I actually started writing this book while sitting in my son's school library shadowing him to help him find some stability).

Yes, our lot is unique and often not understood by those who haven't walked in our shoes.

The upside is that our community is filled with incredibly strong parents; with people who have huge hearts and unmatched stamina. We fight for our children's rights and selflessly put their needs first. This, of course, does frequently result in us becoming over-stretched, isolated and exhausted, so we need to put in some counter-measures to bring balance back to ourselves. I want to help parents like myself feel more balanced and centered as they maintain their ability to thrive.

Exercise:

What are your greatest daily challenges?

_____
_____
_____
_____
_____
_____
_____

Do the different challenges show up at different times in the day?

_____
_____
_____
_____
_____
_____
_____

What strategies, if any, do you incorporate to support yourself with your current challenges?

_____
_____
_____
_____
_____
_____
_____

When do you have time for you? When you do, how do you like to spend it?

_____
_____
_____
_____
_____
_____
_____

How much of this time is spent in conscious self-care?

_____

_____

_____

_____

_____

_____

_____

_____

Is it enough?!

☐ Yes
☐ No

When you did this exercise did you discover that your time spent handling daily challenges outweighs your time spent in replenishment? If so you are not alone. However, as you move through this book allow yourself to discover new ways to bring focus to nurturing yourself.

Self-care doesn't have to be about spending hours 'doing' something to make ourselves feel better, as the reality is we don't have hours each day to sit around contemplating our navels. It is more about spending focused time in short 10-minute bursts, shifting our internal compass so that we create different reactions to the same daily challenges. The result is that we create a different chemical reaction reducing negative stress and bringing more balance to our emotions. Even short moments of self-care increase our energy levels and soothe our monkey minds allowing for the possibility of deeper healing and increased peace in our world. Yet it takes time to change old habits, so be gentle with yourself, support yourself by setting aside at least ten minutes in the morning and evening to try the exercises in the book. When you find ones that you 'LOVE' and that make a positive impact, then chose to incorporate these more into your daily routine, sprinkling them throughout your day. You will find your friends and family starting to ask- "What are you doing to look so good?" Or, "Have you lost weight?" Or, "Did you get your hair done?" I know this to be true, for I have heard this reported to me so often. Don't try to convert such people on the spot, just invite them to visit my site and read the book and then allow them to discover what techniques work best for them.

4

There's a Saber-Toothed Tiger in the Living Room!

There is only one corner of the universe you can be certain of improving, and that's your own self.

Aldous Huxley - late renowned English Author

Our bodies are hard-wired to automatically react to what we **perceive as stressful.** So if our beloved child has a massive overwhelm in the living room because his favorite television show just got canceled or you just ran out of chicken nuggets on nugget night, then our autonomic nervous system, which controls our response to stress, can be triggered in the exact same way as it once did when we were actually at risk from being eaten by a Saber-Toothed Tiger.

This primitive response, a throwback to the time of cave men and actual life threatening animal attacks, is a protection mechanism that you will have heard about called the fight- or-flight response. It's designed to keep us safe. Although we now live in a modernized world where it is no longer essential to "hunt" for our own dinner, our body's initial reaction in a stressful situation, such as our child's massive overwhelm, still harkens back to these primal roots.

As our body prepares itself to respond to the stressor, we become more mentally alert, our hearing and eyesight sharpen. Our digestive system shuts down because we sense it is less important to eat or digest food than to funnel this energy into other systems when we are in protection mode. To increase its strength, the body takes blood from the digestive organs and channels it to the large muscles of the legs and arms; now we can mobilize faster. Blood begins to thicken for faster injury repair. Breathing quickens and becomes shallower. The heart rate and blood pressure increase to pump blood faster to large muscle groups. Adrenaline is released to fuel the need for increased speed. We sweat to cool our bodies to ensure we don't overheat in case we have to go through some major exertion like avoiding the sharp incisors of that tiger!

Flight or Fight stages

- Mentally alert
- Senses sharpen
- Digestion stops
- Blood thickens
- Muscles tense
- Breathing quickens
- Adrenaline released
- Heart rate & blood pressure rise
- Sweat cools the body

Not all stress is bad. In fact stress can be good. It motivates us and gives us the adrenaline needed to win a race, to complete a project to deadline, to get the house cleaned before our in-laws arrive.

Yet too much stress is destructive. John Bradshaw, renowned author and psychotherapist, in his book *Homecoming: Reclaiming and Championing Your Inner Child*, states that: "Adaptation to stress was intended by nature to be a temporary state. It was never intended to be chronic." (Bradshaw 1992)

The problem with stress occurs when the situation causing you to be in this heightened state does not dissipate or go away; when you cannot escape from the tiger or bring him home as your latest feast! That is when we feel overwhelmed and symptoms of negative stress begin to manifest. When you are already in an exhausted state because you've been dealing with constant demands all day at home and/or at the office, then the added strain of helping your child feed himself, or toilet, or recover from a tantrum, or do homework can be the straw that breaks the camel's back.

Another contributor to stress can be the lack of stimulation or repetitive tasks. Boredom affects our stress levels and so getting back to balance is the optimum goal. As all parents of special kids know, there is often a lot of repetition in our daily lives, as well as the possibility for overwhelm depending on the challenges our children are facing.

Even the simple tasks of dressing, feeding, getting your child to school or out of the house for an appointment can be stressful in many ways.

I have often had parents make remarks about the fact that I was late for a play date. They didn't see the hours of preparation it took just to get there. Herding cats is easier then getting my children out of the house.

If I try and 'rush' them by informing them we need to get in the car now to be on time, this can trigger my eldest into a panic attack. He can start screaming, running, banging off walls, hitting himself in the head, refusing to go, because I am causing him stress. Even when I start prepping him two hours in advance that we will be leaving and what will be required of him at the time and he seems agreeable, it can all change - going pear shaped at the last minute.

Then when my eldest eventually calms, my younger son, who I will have asked to go outside or play in another room so he is away from the tantrum, will still have absorbed some of the stress and be frustrated because he is now late for his play date. He will often then start shouting at his just calm brother, about being late for his friends and it's his brother's fault etc. As you can imagine the cycle can start all over again. Oh, yes, my friends if you are reading this you may have had similar experiences.

Those that have witnessed these events are never the friends to comment on me being late ☺ . They are usually ready to present me with a Nobel Peace Prize for patience in the face of extreme adversity.

Sometimes tasks are stressful because of their repetitive nature, but more often, stress results because those duties are physically or emotionally challenging: you must lift your child, or figure out how to maneuver a chair through a busy store, or deal with overwhelm on a daily basis because any change in routine can affect your child's behavior.

Then add to this the stress that we can feel as parents if our child overwhelms or makes a scene in an inappropriate way while we are out in public. Later in Chapter 9 I will explore some powerful tools to help bring balance to your life if dealing with daily overwhelm is a common occurrence, as it is in mine.

Being in a place in our daily life where we feel excited about life, stimulated and engaged yet not over stretched is the objective. Getting there is what this book is about. The truth is we can't control anyone else in our lives but ourselves, we can't change our beloved children; however, we can change our reactions, add new tools to our life skills tool box and set simple manageable goals that have a lasting impact.

The graph below illustrates this point.

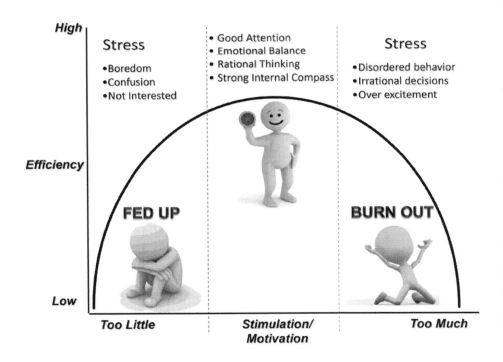

Stress Assessment Stress Graph

Exercise:

Take a moment to assess your life in general or if you wish you can repeat the assessment, to be specific about the different areas that are important to you.

For example: You may find that your home life is different from your work life. Don't forget to date it so you can check back and see how much you have changed; this is a great motivator to continue on the thrive pathway!

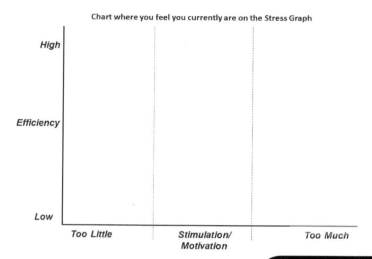

Chart where you feel you currently are on the Stress Graph

Stress Graph Self-Assessment Exercise **download available at ThriveNowToolkit.com**

The truth with this exercise is that you will always shift between different parts of the graph. However if you can allow yourself to stay more in the middle of the graph where you feel more productive in your day and engaged while managing your stress levels, then this is your ideal.

The key is to be gentle on yourself, avoiding the **'shoulds'** and **'musts'** (we will talk about this more in chapter 8) so that life is more in flow with you and your personal and family goals not what you believe you **'should'** be creating because society is reflecting to you an ideal world via the media or community.

Our journey as special parents is unique, our journey is precious and often challenging, yet sometimes deeply rewarding if we let go and embrace the moment in which small miracles can happen.

For example this weekend I had arranged a playdate for my son with his best friend to go to the beach. He totally freaked out – suddenly the beach was enemy number one. Too much sand, cold water, sun too bright, no technology – I was the most hated person on the planet for ruining his life and creating this overwhelm. A very challenging moment as he became very aggressive with me and verbally abusive. I had been so excited to arrange what I had thought would be an exciting adventure yet to him it sounded closer to a hell date.

I walked away from him, I was in full fight or flight mode, I could feel it in my body. I asked for divine support surrounding myself with God's love and light and I started a gratitude practice in that moment. Gratitude for all the times my son was generous, loving and caring towards me. I was grateful for his presence on the earth, for the gifts he was here to share, for my ability to be his mother. I took deep conscious breaths. Now this was not easy as I was very upset, with tears streaming down my face, yet as I continued I could feel my body begin to relax, I could feel my emotions calm. I sent love to my son and blessed him.

Within fifteen minutes my son was back at my side. This time he was kissing my head and apologizing for being so mean. He even went to the beach later where there was a festival and he ended up practicing to walk on a tight rope, dance to the drumming and had a wonderful time with his best friend.

This flight or fight response in the body is an automatic response controlled by the autonomic nervous system in the body. The autonomic nervous system has two parts, the sympathetic nervous system and the parasympathetic nervous system.

They work in tandem almost like a see-saw. The sympathetic nervous system (SNS) stimulates the body, calling forth the body to increase energy output, while the parasympathetic nervous system (PNS) decreases these responses by creating counter measures to the initial flight or fight. When something happens that you **perceive** as stressful, a message is instantaneously sent to the brain. This automatic action sends out a call to action to all the body and the flight or fight response is the result.

However the PNS cannot return the body to a full relaxation response instantaneously. The body can begin restoring itself within as quickly as three minutes; however, full restoration may take as long as **twenty minutes.** In our natural state, the physical action of running from the sabre tooth tiger or clubbing him to bring him home for dinner released the stress response and rebalanced our PNS naturally. (You can see how road rage can develop!)

In modern society we cannot go around clubbing our bosses or running out of a store if our child starts to embarrass us by overwhelming. Yet this is the body's natural response and the stress is trapped in our systems unless we consciously use different tools and techniques to bring ourselves back to balance. We will explore many different ways to do this simply and easily.

Researchers from the University of Wisconsin-Madison have gauged the impact that parenting a special needs child can have on our stress levels. For eight consecutive days, researchers followed a group of mothers whose offspring were either adolescents or adults with autism. The researchers conducted daily interviews with each Mom about her experiences, and took their hormone levels mid-way through the eight days to assess their stress chemical balance. (Marsha Mailick Seltzer 2009)

The results were shocking; **hormone levels were consistent with people experiencing chronic stress. The researchers compared the mothers' blood work to that of soldiers in combat—and found their levels similar.**

> *"This is the physiological residue of daily stress," says Marsha Mailick Seltzer, who authored the studies. "The mothers of children with high levels of behavior problems have the most pronounced physiological profile of chronic stress, but the long-term effect on their physical health is not yet known."*

The ongoing events and responsibilities of parenting a special needs child can result in our bodies never recovering from a stress response, and if we have the compounding effect of one after another, we could potentially feel stressed all of the time as illustrated in the graph on next page:

Of course balancing our own stress isn't just good for us; it is also good for those we live and work with, and especially for our super sensitive children.

Stress Level

A rapid stress response requires an extended period to release this stress from our body.

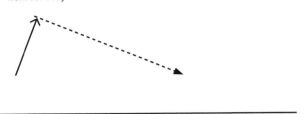

Time

Stress Level

During a "regular" Special Needs Parenting day we can easily come across multiple stress inducing situations, to put it mildly!

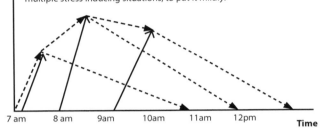

7 am   8 am   9am   10am   11am   12pm

Time

Stress Level

If we don't turn our focus to reducing our stress levels after we experience the response, our day turns into one long period of stress.

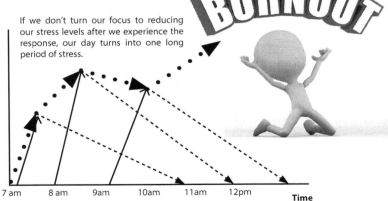

7 am   8 am   9am   10am   11am   12pm

Time

Exercise:

As you read this chapter what emotions or thoughts did you have? Just becoming aware of your reactions and inner feelings are healing for the body. Please take a moment to reflect. This is a foundational skill for taking control of your stress responses and we will look at ways to build on this further in the book.

_____

_____

_____

_____

_____

_____

_____

_____

_____

_____

_____

_____

_____

_____

_____

_____

_____

_____

_____

_____

_____

_____

_____

5

Stress Awareness for Super Heroes!

"To bring up a child in the way he should go, travel that way yourself once in a while."

Henry Wheeler Shaw - 19th century American humorist (1818 –1885)

*M*y son is very sensitive. He has told me 'Mommy I feel everyone's pain when I walk into a room".

This is a challenge. However, in my experience this phenomenon is common among children on the autism spectrum, as it is with other special needs children. I have heard many similar stories from other parents. How their child "channels" everyone's emotions in a room and presents it to the group, to put it mildly! On one occasion, I brought my son to a neighbor's house for a party. Upon walking in, I noticed an uneasy feeling as if someone had been fighting before we arrived. My son lasted all of two minutes, screamed and ran out of the front door waving his arms and running at full speed back home.

Given the ultra-sensitive nature of my son, it is exceptionally important for me to take time to center myself as regularly as possible in order to avoid having him experience unnecessary stress that is not even his! What if you were to take this sensitivity in your child as a given? What, then, could you do for yourself to release your stress so you can feel better for more of your day, while also helping your child feel more aligned each day? What a great deal that would be!

Of course being super sensitive is not just true of special needs children. More than fifteen years ago I was hosting a new workshop series, "Self-care for Single Moms". A wonderful group of women attended. Most felt overwhelmed by their daily demands and financial hardships. I had the pleasure to be able to work with this group over a six-week period for three hours each week.

We had such fun—giggling, crying and transforming during that time. All the moms felt dramatically more balanced even after the second week, which is what I had hoped would happen. On the third week, they arrived at class with the same big grins and asked;

"What are you doing to our kids?"

They went on to explain that, since they had started the training, their children were all calmer, more compliant and so much easier to be with. As a joke they were surmising that I must be breaking into their homes and feeding their children happy pills!

I assured them that my ninja skills were rusty; however, I was fascinated to hear more from them about what they had experienced, as this was an unexpected benefit. Because I wasn't a mother yet I hadn't developed any preconceived idea that this might be a **Side Effect** of the training workshop. I was really excited and energized to find that each woman reported the same findings.

When I asked them if they had any insights, one teary mom said her teenager had told her "Mom you are happier, you don't shout at me all the time, I like being around you." Everyone else's eyes started to glisten as they nodded to confirm that similar responses were coming from their kids too.

Over the next few years, I continued to work with similar groups of parents and ALL reported the same findings. Eventually I began to list the changes in the participants' children as a benefit of the workshop.

When parents take the time to focus on themselves positively—consciously relaxing, choosing to shift gears into a slower lane and making positive life skill choices—the change affects those nearest and dearest to them, their children and spouses.

When I started to research this finding, I found that I wasn't the first to discover this and that research into parents' stress levels and how it impacted their children's behavior and state of mind went as far back as the 1950s.

Award-winning author and Episcopal minister, David Code, in his book *Kids Pick Up on Everything: How Parental Stress is Toxic to Kids*, writes: "children become barometers for their parents' state of mind.... Kids pick up on everything, especially our stress and anxiety." He goes on to say: "This is not the mother's or father's fault. Today's parents are more stressed-out because our social support networks are dwindling, and we don't realize that, as our isolation increases, it drives up our stress levels." (Code 2011)

Of course, to start being able to manage your stress levels, you need to figure out how stress is actually affecting you.

When I first started on this journey at the age of twenty-four, I was unconscious of the different ways that stress was affecting me. I had suffered from total stress burnout that shot my adrenal glands. I was only aware of exhaustion and physical pain that had become my daily existence. Yet stress affects us all differently and it impacts different areas of our lives – physically, emotionally, mentally, spiritually and within our relationships.

On the next page is a **Stress Exhaustion Symptom List** to help you uncover how stress may be impacting your life. It is the first step in developing awareness so that change is possible.

Don't panic if, when you do this exercise, you have nearly all the items ticked. When I began this journey, I filled in nearly every box and I am now in a place of much greater wellness than I thought was possible at that time.

The key is **AWARENESS**. This is the first step in change, for without awareness nothing new is possible. Awareness isn't always comfortable. At first you might even feel like your stress levels are increasing. Trust me, they are not. It is just that you are becoming conscious of your stress responses and the **patterns that are running you**.

Exercise:

Please tick the stress exhaustion symptoms you are aware of experiencing in the last two months. (This is a great exercise to share with your close friend and/or partner).

Stress Exhaustion Symptoms

Physical

- Fatigue
- Tension
- Headaches
- Teeth grinding
- Muscles aches
- Muscle tension
- Digestive upsets
- Heart palpitations
- Being more clumsy
- Foot or finger drumming
- Increased sugar cravings
- Constipation or diarrhea
- Immune issues, e.g. more colds
- Insomnia or change in sleep patterns
- Increased coffee, alcohol or tobacco use
- Appetite change – increase or decrease
- Weight change either increase or decrease

Emotional

- Anxiety
- Worrying
- Irritability
- Frustration
- Nightmares
- Depression
- Mood swings
- Bad temper
- Crying spells
- Feeling 'blue'
- Nervous Laughter
- Easily discouraged
- Feeling like no-one cares
- Finding little to be joyful about

Spiritual

- Apathy
- Doubt
- Martyrdom
- Emptiness
- Loss of direction
- Loss of meaning
- Inability to forgive
- Looking for magic
- Needing to 'prove' yourself
- Feeling disconnected from purpose

Mental

- Boredom
- Lethargy
- Confusion
- Spacing out
- Whirling mind
- Forgetfulness
- Dulled senses
- Low productivity

- [ ] Negative self-talk
- [ ] Negative attitude
- [ ] Difficulty focusing
- [ ] Poor concentration
- [ ] Memory issues, e.g. forgetting what you went up stairs for

Within Relationships

- [ ] Hiding
- [ ] Distrust
- [ ] Nagging
- [ ] Isolation
- [ ] Intolerance
- [ ] Resentment
- [ ] Loneliness
- [ ] Lashing out
- [ ] Using people
- [ ] Clamming up
- [ ] Lack of intimacy
- [ ] Lowered sex drive
- [ ] Fewer contacts with friends

As I mentioned before, setting ourselves simple and achievable goals helps us develop awareness and create lasting change in our daily lives. This section is to support you - optional but highly recommended. Fill in the date after the word **week** so you can monitor your progress.

Weekly Goal:

Between NOW and this date: ___/___/___, I choose to develop awareness around my stress symptoms and to record the main ones I notice.

_____
_____
_____
_____
_____
_____

Benefit from achieving this goal

_____
_____
_____

Negative outcome if not achieved. Be honest with yourself

_____
_____
_____
_____

How I feel now that I've achieved this goal! ☺

_____
_____
_____
_____

6

The Secret of Healthy-Self-Love

"Knowing others is intelligence; knowing yourself is true wisdom. Mastering others is strength; mastering yourself is true power."
Lao Tzu, 6th Century BC Classic Chinese Author

*a*s I mentioned in the previous chapter, I began the journey toward recovering my health, after burning out from stress at the early age of twenty-four. At that point, I believed that I had burnt out purely because I had been in a job that didn't suit me, and that the company had overworked me. I felt like a victim and at some level it felt good to have someone to blame for my sickness.

What I came to realize was that I loved to live in drama and that making myself the victim and the big company the bad guy really felt good somewhere deep inside. It also meant, of course, that I was not fully responsible for my illness. Others had done this to me - my boss who loved to bully me, my co-workers who had left, and the company that would not hire replacements for them. Poor me!

However, when I began working with a stress management consultant, what I discovered shocked me. I realized quickly that although I *had* burnt-out from working too hard, the real cause was that I felt I had to work that hard because I was not worthy enough to decline/refuse the extra workload.

- I had never said NO!
- I had never stopped to think about me!
- I didn't really know what my own gifts were!
- I had put everyone else's needs ahead of my own!

I also had to face the fact that my self-esteem had taken a beating and I didn't really have any self-care skills. My way to avoid stress was to withdraw or put my head down and work more. I ate too much junk food, smoked cigarettes, drank six to eight cups of coffee a day and partied too hard at the weekends. I drank barely any water and after being an athlete in school, I now viewed exercise as an elusive thing I knew 'I should' do, but couldn't seem to fit it in.

When I analyzed my habits I realized that although I had learned many things throughout my life I had not grown up in a culture that had valued self-care. I didn't know how to honor myself or manage my stress. I knew nothing about what really mattered—creating balance.

As part of my journey of rebuilding my health and well-being, I enrolled in a self-esteem building class for women. This class was very powerful and transformational. This next exercise to outline personal achievements and successes to date, was a particularly powerful one for me at the time and I hope you find it helpful also. I found it challenging at first but once I moved into the flow of honoring myself, words and feelings began to pour out. Eventually I discovered that loving myself was actually easier then beating myself up constantly for not being good enough. It took less energy and had much nicer results!

According to psychology, self-esteem is a person's overall sense of self-worth or personal value. I discovered that my self-esteem was an accumulation of beliefs that I had created about how I perceived myself and how I believed others saw me. Like everyone else's beliefs, mine were formed beginning in childhood and into adulthood, created from self-perception and messages generated by and absorbed from the world around me—family, culture, community, media, friends and colleagues. In my case these beliefs had resulted in me not valuing my true worth. They allowed me to martyr myself, to overwork myself, to over-care for the company I worked for, at the expense of my own needs and health.

“The worst loneliness is to not be comfortable with yourself.”
Mark Twain (1835-1910) American Author and Humorist

Exercise 1:

Yes I actually am a Super Hero!!

Sit with a piece of paper and a full box of toothpicks or matches. Begin thinking about your life to this date and make a note of all **the incredible things** that you have achieved.

TIP: Start with small successes. I have found that living with a special needs child really helped me reframe the supposedly simple tasks that many take for granted. Take nothing for granted, honor all success and achievements, small and large. For example when I did this I started with: I learnt to crawl; I learnt to walk; I was able to feed myself, etc. Then you may build up to more adult oriented success.

For every remembered success, pick a match from the box and watch the pile grow high. We so often discard our successes, moving quickly onto the next challenge or hurdle in front of us, or just focusing on what we think we did wrong.

See if you can reach 100 items. Take note if you feel yourself thinking "I can't" or "I'm not good enough." If this happens take a few deep breaths and tell yourself: "I am worth it", "I am special", "I grow stronger everyday." Or pick another statement that works for you.

Also, take note of any other negative talk that your mind presents; we will be looking at this in-depth, later in the book.

_____

_____

_____

_____

_____

_____

_____

_____

Take a moment to note how **you felt during this exercise.** Did you write with ease and grace? Did you feel frustration and anger? Or some feeling in between? Again, you are developing awareness as to what triggers you and stimulates you. Value all of these new insights like gold pieces. Record each feeling below!

Also notice if you discovered any negative beliefs as you were working on the previous exercise. Did you recognize anyone's voice? Often we can hear one of our parents, or someone else in a position of authority. Just take note of the name, and we will look in more depth at such voices in Chapter 8.

_____

_____

_____

_____

_____

_____

_____

_____

Exercise 2:

Read your extensive list and put a star next to your top three achievements. Which successes make you feel most proud of yourself, most expansive?

Remember these do not have to be mammoth successes like climbing Mount Everest. I once worked with a beautiful mother who was recovering from an eight-year long addiction to heroin. Her greatest sense of success was sitting with her children watching television! Just doing that made her feel connected and present in a way she had not felt during her past eight years. When she went to this simple place in her mind, she visibly lit up. She felt proud of herself and could feel the difference inside.

In this exercise, as you begin to look at the common thread between your top three achievements, you may find clues about what really stimulates and motivates you in life. Often when we have experienced ongoing chronic stress, we feel separated from our past successes. Our accomplishments feel like distant memories of a life before . . . .

However, this doesn't have to be the case. When you realize what exactly was the most stimulating and expansive aspect of your top success, you have an opportunity to find activities that once again can create those good feelings in you on a more regular basis.

What do your top three achievements have in common?

_____
_____
_____
_____
_____
_____
_____

What could you do to allow these feelings of success back into your life?

_____
_____
_____
_____
_____
_____
_____

"Passion is energy. Feel the power that comes from focusing on what excited you."

Oprah Winfrey (1950 – to date); American media proprietor,
talk show host, actress, producer, and philanthropist

Exercise 3:

This exercises uses your ability to access memories to create a powerful, personalized visualization. This is a tool that you can use at anytime to release those feel good endorphins .

Start by choosing your top achievement or point of success. Then follow the instructions below to re-create this experience. We store memories in different ways. For some of us, the memory will be mostly visual. Others may have stored that experience as sensation, as how and what we felt. For some sounds will predominate in memory, or perhaps smells, or colors.

Tip: Close your eyes for a moment and bring the event into your mind. What were you wearing? Who were you with? What was the setting? What colors were there? What sounds, textures and smells? Recreate the occasion as fully as you can. Notice how your body feels different during this experience of recreation. Notice how it feels afterwards. Just thinking about a successful event can create a visceral experience in the body. Take note of whether this happened for you. Stay here as long as you wish enjoying the experience. Returning to write your notes on how this felt for you and what you experienced when you are ready.

_____
_____
_____
_____
_____
_____
_____
_____
_____
_____
_____
_____
_____
_____
_____
_____
_____
_____
_____
_____

Weekly Goal:

Between NOW and this date: ___/___/___, I choose to develop awareness around focusing on my successes everyday, even the smallest ones. You might note that you managed to shower and buy the groceries. Your successes should predominate, not your perceived challenges and failures!

_____
_____
_____
_____
_____
_____

Benefit from achieving this goal

_____
_____
_____
_____
_____

Negative outcome if not achieved – be honest with yourself

_____
_____
_____
_____
_____

How I feel now that I've achieved this goal! ☺

_____
_____
_____
_____
_____

7

Energy Management

"Most people spend more time and energy going around problems than in trying to solve them."
Henry Ford (1863 –1947) an American industrialist

O n my journey to improved health and self-esteem, I had another huge realization: I was losing much of my energy to others. As I strengthened my self-esteem using exercises from the previous chapter I also looked at where I was focusing my energy on a daily basis. When I brought this aspect of my life into awareness I was surprised by how little control I had felt I had over my own experiences and how tiring being 'out of control' was.

I was blaming others for outcomes in my life as I did with my stress burn out. I was putting much of my energy into situations in my past over which I no longer had any control. I was 'wasting energy' replaying old arguments. "Oh I wish I had thought of that at the time," or "Why didn't I say that?" This was both disempowering and exhausting.

In the last exercise, you recreated in your mind a successful event; your energy will have lifted from doing this. Now imagine how your body responds when you spend much of your time in a place of blaming others or victimhood. Yes, just as contemplating your success had a real-life visceral effect, unfortunately so does a negative focus.

For me I really needed to become aware of this again after my son had an allergic reaction to his first vaccine. I was angry, terrified, distraught, wishing to blame, wishing to fight, yet my training had thought me that this way of being won't change what had happened to my son. Blaming and anger wouldn't reverse time to before the vaccine where I could refuse to have it administered, it would only increase my stress levels and reduce my health levels. My thoughts and reactions needed to not be that of a victim but to come from a place of reality and empowerment. The truth is many children have vaccines and don't have allergic reactions to them, but my son did. At six weeks old I didn't realize that Oisin would respond this way, I couldn't blame myself, I couldn't blame the makers of the vaccine, I couldn't blame the doctors or nurses, I couldn't blame my son. It just was and I needed to deal with the current reality not from the **what if** place, but from the empowered space of **what now** space. I needed to consciously change.

In a recent article in *Psychology Today,* Doctor Raj Raghunathan, Ph.D, reported that when business students where asked to observe their thoughts and be 'brutally honest' over a two-week period the findings showed that 60 and 70 percent of the average students spontaneously occurring thoughts are negative. This is one of many studies that reveal similar results. It shows that our 'mental chatter' or 'monkey mind' is mostly (up to seventy percent) negative, a phenomenon that is sometimes referred to as negativity dominance. (Doctor Raj Raghunathan 2013)

Also, it seems that we are not responsible for our first thought in a situation as this is totally unconscious. However that's where our "Get out of jail free" card ends. We have the ability to counterbalance every thought after the first automatic one.

The only way to be successful in retraining our thoughts is to develop awareness of what they are in the first place. When I begin working with clients they sometimes think they are getting more stressed. However this is not the case. What they soon realize is that they are just becoming aware of all the underlying patterns that have been running their lives unconsciously. This usually comes as a shock.

They are not more stressed, just more aware, and although at first this can feel uncomfortable, without this newly developed awareness it is impossible to become truly empowered. This is the starting point of beginning to control stress levels and being able to increase health and well-being.

A quick way to check your thoughts is to turn off background noise. For example, I often drive with no radio playing so I can hear my thoughts. Often we chose to drown out our internal chatter by keeping our minds busy listening to music, watching TV, or reading. Yet if we consciously sit and just tune inwards several times a day, listening to what we are saying to ourselves, most of us will quickly begin to see a pattern of self-talk. In the previous chapter we looked at how self-esteem is a compilation of beliefs absorbed from our perceptions of how others feel about us. When we begin to develop awareness of our internal self-talk we can often here the same voices that were involved in creating of our sense of self-worth.

You may even be aware that there are a number of voices speaking to you. Perhaps you hear the voices of your parents, teachers or an old friend. The secret is to observe and take note so you can make adjustments to this internal chatter, a process we will discuss later in Chapter 8.

Now I want you to bring awareness to the places where you are losing your energy on a daily basis. The next exercise will explore this in more detail.

Exercise:
My "Energetic" Bank Account

Imagine your energy levels are like a bank account and every day you wake up with it full. Let's call that amount $10,000. Now imagine that often before you get out of bed you have already depleted your account down to $1,000.

Deposits get withdrawn because

$1,500 = you are frustrated with the school system and how it is treating your child,
$1,500 = you feel anger toward your partner for something they did or didn't do,
$1,000= you replay an old festering argument with a family member or friend,
$2,000 = you worry over an upcoming event,
$3,000 = you beat yourself up for getting that speeding ticket and for not saying the clever one liner you "should" have said to the officer at the time (even though it was five months ago).
$9,000 = Depleted Energy before even getting out of bed

Then as you move through your day, handling your daily concerns, balancing work, paying bills, managing the household, supporting your child or children by mid-morning, you may be overdrawn!

If this is the case, then in reality the energy you use for the rest of the day will be drawn from your vital organs' reserves and if this pattern continues over a long period, it can result in chronic health issues as I discovered myself, where I totally burned out my adrenal glands and created chronic fatigue for myself.

When I had my big light bulb moment with this and realized that I could take charge of my own energy, I started to turn my life around. The external world did not change at first. I still had no job. I still had little money. I still was ill. Yet *how* I began to feel about such issues was different, for a light was turned on inside of me.

Awareness is the key so lets explore where you are losing your energy!

Answers these questions:
Where are you focusing your energy today? Are you focusing more on the past, the present or worrying about the future?

_____

_____

_____

Who are you giving your energy away to? Old arguments, blaming others, feeling victimized, worrying about your child!

_____

_____

_____

How are you replenishing yourself? What self-care skills and good nutrition are you investing in during your day to maintain your energy and revitalize your body?

_____

_____

_____

In truth we all have energy drains in our lives. We never feel 'happy' and full of energy all the time. Life always has ups and downs. Otherwise, how would we know what an up feeling is if we have never had a down feeling. However, when we become more aware of where we lose energy and hold resistance, it empowers up to make a choice.

We can choose to stay in that energy or choose to release it and move forward, giving us the ability to have a different reaction and thus a different experience. I can't 'change' the way my son overwhelms when I am out in a crowd with him; but I can react calmly or I can react with stress. It's my choice. And that very reaction impacts him directly. His overwhelm can escalate and continue to full panic where he loses control completely or he may notice my sense of calm and realize that his panic mightn't be as necessary as he thought.

Exercise:

Read the list below and see what fits your energy profile! Don't try to be 'RIGHT.' Be honest with yourself; no-one is looking over your shoulder.

You Lose energy through:

Fear
Grief
Anger
Blame
Stress
Revenge
Victimhood
Frustration
Lack of sleep
Lack of exercise
Poor self-image
Negative self-talk
Poor diet & nutrition
Too much alcohol & smoking
Too much concern about others
 (add your own)

You Maintain Energy through:

- Spending fun time with friends
- Positively expressing emotions
- Having a goal or ambition
- Happiness & laughter
- Good quality sleep
- Healthy eating
- Spiritual practice
- Positive self-talk
- Keeping a journal
- Having a pet to stroke
- Regular exercise that you enjoy
- Balanced nutritional supplements
- Incorporating new activities into your daily routine
- Self-nurturing—e.g. getting a massage, soaking in a bath
- Working with a coach or therapist to support transformation
- Attending workshops online or in person to stimulate and engage you
- Relaxation techniques such as deep breathing, meditation (see Chapter 12)
- (add your own)

Take note of any awareness that came to you during this exercise, including areas where you felt resistance, and areas where you felt positive.

_____
_____
_____
_____
_____
_____
_____
_____
_____
_____
_____
_____

Weekly Goal:

Between NOW and this date: ___/___/___, I choose to let go of one energy drainer which is

_____

_____

_____

I will replace it with one energy maintainer which is

_____

_____

_____

The benefit for me in achieving this goal is

_____

_____

_____

The negative outcome if I do not achieve this goal is

_____

_____

_____

_____

This is how I feel after achieving this goal: ☺

_____

_____

_____

Don't forget to post your commitment on Facebook and tell close friends or family so they can support you in your transformation!

8

I Am What I Think! Letting Go of Old Toxic Patterns

"He that is good for making excuses is seldom good for anything else."
Benjamin Franklin (1706-1790)–
visionary & Founding Father of the USA

I know most people say you are what you eat, and I totally agree. You will see I have a whole chapter on healthy eating and nutrition later in the book. However, it has been my experience over the years that what most dramatically impacts our stress levels is our self-talk, the internal language we use each day.

I blogged one day about one of my favorite kid's book *The Little Engine That Could* and the power of this message. The messages we send to ourselves are fundamental to our health. How we speak to ourselves – whether we encourage and support ourselves or diminish our energy— determines whether we get up and move forward or sit back in a sense of lack and limitation. Psychologists call this "Intrapersonal Communication" or 'Self-Talk'.

You might want to sit back and think: "Am I like the little blue engine or more like the other trains that came and went, making excuses for their inability to try?"

According to a research article written by Julia E. Weikle in 1993, "Self-talk is a health behavior that has potentially far-reaching effects. Although it will most likely be used by those who have a high internal locus of control and place a high value on health, it can also help relatively healthy people in health 'maintenance' programs." (Weikle 1993)

So many psychologists and medical professionals have researched the link between mind and body health. The ancient religions such as Buddhism also have mindfulness and emotion regulation at the center of their core beliefs.

In his *Path to Tranquility: Daily Wisdom*, the Dalai Lama writes, "If there is love, there is hope to have real families, real brotherhood, real equanimity, real peace. If the love within your mind is lost, if you continue to see other beings as enemies, then no matter how much knowledge or education you have, no matter how much material progress is made, only suffering and confusion will ensue." (Lama 1998)

Growing up, I was never taught this wisdom. I was never asked to observe my thoughts and analyze how my body reacted to them and whether love was present in my reactions. Self-study never seemed to be on the agenda, and after working with thousands of clients, I realized I wasn't the only one who had never been invited to create this powerful life skill.

I took my own power back into my life when I became able to control the direction of my thoughts. The results were incredible. In brief, my health levels increased, my relationships improved, my stress levels reduced, which increased my energy levels. And honestly, I was a much nicer person to be with!

"Almost every minute of your conscious life you are engaging in self-talk, your internal thought language. These are the sentences with which you describe and interpret the world. If the self-talk is accurate and in touch with reality, you function well. If it is irrational and untrue, then you experience stress and emotional disturbance." This truth about the power of our internal dialogue with ourselves appears in *The Relaxation & Stress Reduction Workbook* by psychologists Martha Davis, PH.D. Elizabeth Robbins Eshelman M.S.W, & Matthew McKay PH.D. (Martha Davis 2007)

When we think about a situation that is creating stressful feelings for us, remember: We are not responsible for our first thought in that moment, as this is an automatic response. However every thought after that we can bring our awareness, and then choose to have a different reaction.

Before we can generate compassion and love, it is important to have a clear understanding of what we understand compassion and love to be. In simple terms, compassion and love can be defined as positive thoughts and feelings that give rise to such essential things in life as hope, courage, determination, and inner strength.

His Holiness the 14th Dalai Lama, (1935 – present)
from *The Compassionate Life*

What we think has a direct impact on our stress levels and our emotional response in situations. A quick way of figuring out if your thoughts are not serving you is to notice how you are feeling. Tension, anxiety, fear, anger, increased pain levels, over reactivity are all indications that your mind is probably not serving you at that moment. Just by bringing awareness to the foremost thought creating your emotional response is enough to start to change it.

Awareness is everything. If our thoughts go unchecked they run in the background of our mind like a tape or CD on repeat. Observing them allows us to start changing the program and adding our own conscious beliefs that can fundamentally empower us to increase health and well-being.

As stated before, our unconscious thoughts are usually not just our own, they are a collection gathered from many places –
- Our family
- Our peers
- Our community
- Our past experiences.
- Our culture and heritage
- Mass media – television, cinema, internet, radio, print etc.

We in turn pass these belief systems onto our children and those around us. I often outline this to my clients by asking them to imagine they are wearing glasses. The lenses of these glasses are made up of every past experience and absorbed belief system they have had.

I point out to them that if this is the case then couldn't their perceived reaction in a situation be just that, a perceived response, not necessarily based on the true fact of the situation but a multiple layered reaction to an event actually triggered, not just by the actual facts of the event, but by how they view the world through their own unique lenses.

A.   **B.**   **C.**

Event ----->Beliefs about the event---->Emotional response (includes self-talk)

A does not cause C, B does. How we **PERCEIVE** a situation and the belief that underlies that perception play a major role in the resulting feelings and our body's reactions.

When an irrational belief is operating, the experience you feel may seem out of proportion to the event itself.
Developing awareness of these belief systems has helped many clients shift perspective and adjust the internal self-talk to help reduce stress levels.

I decided to conduct an experiment, using myself as the guinea pig, in August 2012. I committed to do something that would normally have created a huge amount of fear in me.

I rappelled off the tallest water front building on the West Coast. It was 33 floors, 360 feet tall and I came down the side of it on a rope. By doing so, I raised over $1,200 to support an organization that works with kids with disabilities, Kids Included Together, better known as KIT. You can check out my crazy rappel on my **YouTube Channel Siobhan Wilcox** here is the link http://youtu.be/gtK7-QrRPUA

I found this to be a powerful and educational event. I used certain techniques such as positive self-talk, reframing and deep abdominal breathing to shift my fear coming up to the event. I deeply observed my internal process. What I discovered surprised me.

Every time I would begin to feel fear around this event I would sit in silence and observe the fear and its origin. Often I found the greatest fear was coming from the outside—from my family's and peers' fears of what I was attempting. The fear was actually not my own.

Others were impacting me with their concerns and worries. It was *their* perception that I was absorbing and was taking into my consciousness. I was reacting as if their worries were my true response, when truly they were not. My true response was excitement, expansion, feeling powerful. I believed that doing this rappel would shift my internal compass to a place of positivity and empowerment. And the truth is that it did.

On the day of the event I was excited and felt no fear. Instead I was helping others in my life overcome their fears and shift their internal compasses, too, for they would see and share the sense of power I felt in this accomplishment.

Our Mind and Attitude Creates Either Positive or Negative Self-talk

Sometimes we magnify the negative aspects of a situation, allowing ourselves to swim around in the drama.

We also often personalize bad occurrences, blaming everything on ourselves, even when an event was outside our control. We see this pattern often in children who take on the "blame" for their parents' divorce.

We use catastrophizing words such as **"It's awful,"** or **"It's terrible,"** words that add to our increased stress levels and decrease our sense of power in a situation.

Another way we produce negative self-talk is to see the world as only black or white, right or wrong. I notice this attitude often in my son who is on the autism spectrum. For him, focusing on the subtle nuances in a situation can be challenging; there seems to be no middle ground or gray area.

We use words that set us up for exhaustion and failure, words such as **"I should," "I have to," "I must."**

When we practice a negative belief or self-talk long enough, we create a neurological pattern in our brain. Imagine a loop like a train track. Every time we experience a certain automatic response the neurons react in the same way, forming a deeper track. Every time we experience a similar event, our mind automatically starts on the same neurological loop again, repeating the same thoughts and same negative reactions and secreting the same chemicals.

Consider this wisdom from the film, *What the Bleep Do We Know?*

❝ There's a part of the brain called the hypothalamus, and the hypothalamus is like a little mini factory and it is a place that assembles certain chemicals that matches certain emotions that we experience. And those particular chemicals are called peptides... So there are chemicals for anger, and there are chemicals for sadness, and there are chemicals for victimization... There's a chemical that matches every emotional state that we experience. And the moment that we experience that emotional state in our body or in our brain that hypothalamus will immediately assemble the peptide and then releases it through the pituitary (master gland in the body that controls the endocrine /hormonal system) into the bloodstream. The moment it makes it into the bloodstream it finds its way to different centers or different parts of the body.... And when a peptide docks on a cell it literally, like a key going into a lock, sits on the receptor surface and attaches to it, and kind of moves the receptor. And kind of like a doorbell buzzing, sends a signal into the cell. It creates a buzz in the body.... Heroin uses the same receptor mechanisms on the cells that our emotional chemicals use. It's easy to see then that if we can be addicted to heroin...then we can be addicted to any neural peptide, any emotion. ❞

-(What the Bleep Do We Know? - Down The Rabbit Hole 2006)

If we consider this belief that we can become addicted to emotions that are created fundamentally by our thoughts, we can see how important it is to master our reactions to events and situations.

The UCLA psychiatrist Jeffrey M Schwartz works with patients with Obsessive Compulsive Disorder (OCD), a condition marked by thoughts that create fear and anxiety taken to an extreme level of ritualistic compulsions. Such compulsions reduce the quality of the OCD sufferer's life.

Using PET brain scans Doctor Schwartz was able to observe that OCD patients' brains did not "turn the page." Their brain would get stuck on a particular thought or obsession. Based on the latest findings in science that the brain can change itself—a quality of the brain known as neuroplasticity—Schwartz was able to prove that his patients "could shift the brain 'manually' by paying constant, effortful attention and actively focusing on something beside the worry, such as new, pleasurable activity."
– *The Brain that Changes Itself* by Norman Dodge M.D. (Dodge 2007)

Again using brain scans these techniques where shown to light up new parts of the brain, helping the OCD patient "shift gears" and create new neural pathways and different reactions, reducing the obsessive response.

Even if we do not suffer from OCD, we all have the tendency to "not turn the page" when we repeat the same response to similar stressors in our lives. As Doctor Schwartz proved, refocusing the brain and consciously shifting gears to a happy task and thoughts, shifted the brain and created new neuron connections. If practiced these then become the new train track in the brain that you automatically go too and your stress levels reduce.

Negative Self-talk

Steps to take towards identifying and disputing irrational beliefs:

1. Look at the objective facts of an upsetting event. For example: *My child is overwhelming as I have invited new friends to the house for dinner. He is running around waving his hands and banging himself off the wall, biting his arm.*

2. Write down your self-talk about the event. Include all subjective value judgments, assumptions, beliefs, predictions, and worries. Note which self-statements you have identified as irrational beliefs, such as: *My child is always ruining my life, he is doing this on purpose. I will never be able to have a normal life. It's so exhausting to be in a constant state of managing his overwhelm. I am so exhausted. I wish I could just be sick, then I could get a break and someone else could deal with this mess. My friends are never going to invite us to anything or come back to our house. This is the worst thing that could have happened. Now everyone thinks I'm a rubbish mother, raising a brat. We will never have any community. This is so terrible.*

3. Note your emotional and physical response. For example: *I am so upset and embarrassed. I just want to cry and run away. My body is tired. My body feels beaten up. My shoulders are tense and I'm grinding my jaw. Exhaustion overwhelms me, and I feel depressed. Let me crawl away and go to bed please.*

4. Dispute the belief. For example: *My son is not deliberately trying to ruin my dinner gathering with friends. He is just overwhelmed because of the extra energy and noise that ten people arriving in the house at the same time create. I also felt a little overwhelmed when everyone arrived but I know how to manage my energy better then he can, so if I felt overwhelmed then he is going to as well. These are very nice people and they will understand my son's behavior if I explain to them what is happening. There is no need to feel depressed as this only adds to my sons overwhelm, he needs me to be calm and centered, to show him extra love so he feels safe and he will begin to calm down. I am a really good mother. I always support myself and my son. I am filled with energy and vitality. I am calm and safe; all is good in my world.*

   This is just one incident and the next time I invite these friends over he will be more used to them and he will not overwhelm in this way. I will ask them to come at different times so that ten people don't come through the door all at the same time. If the noise level increases slowly, he will not have the same sensory challenges.

Rules to Promote Rational Thinking

1. It doesn't do anything to me.

2. Everything is exactly the way it "is."

3. All humans are fallible creatures.

4. It takes two to have a conflict.

5. The original cause is lost in antiquity.

6. We feel the way we think.

Working with shifting your internal negative self-talk can take time yet the rewards are many – reduced stressors, less physical stress on the body, improved peace of mind, increased energy levels, calmer reactions – all result in greater quality of life. Again you are not trying to be perfect as this in it's own right adds to your stress and negative impacting beliefs – you are just developing awareness and being gentle on yourself – treating yourself with loving and nurturing actions.

At the www.ThriveNowToolkit.com I have added a bonus section on Positive Affirmations a way to help yourself improve your negative dominance and increase the art of self-love!

Weekly Goal:

Between NOW and this date: ___/___/___, I choose to become aware of one of my negative self-talk patterns.

_____
_____
_____

I will replace it with this positive and more reality based statement:

_____
_____
_____
_____

Benefit to achieving this goal:

_____
_____
_____
_____

Negative outcome if not achieved:

_____
_____
_____
_____

How I feel after achieving this goal ☺

_____
_____
_____
_____

9

Creating Greater Balance

"Live today. Not yesterday. Not tomorrow. Just today. Inhabit your moments. Don't rent them out to tomorrow."
Jerry Spinelli (1941-), Author

To thrive in life requires a tool-kit full of techniques that can support you in your everyday life. Although getting a massage is a great way to relax, and one I recommend as part of a regular self-care plan, the truth is that if you do not have solutions to help heal your emotional and stress induced-responses, then you can never totally find deep relaxation for long, no matter how good your massage therapist is!

In this chapter we will explore a number of simple techniques that can support you. The first is called *Emotional Freedom Technique* (EFT) or Tapping, which is a powerful tool I use to help release stress from my body. Dr. Roger Callahan, an American psychologist who specialized in anxiety disorders, was the first to discover EFT.

In the early 1980s, Dr. Callahan was looking for solutions to help some of his more troubled patients. Along this journey, he studied both Applied Kinesiology and the ancient Chinese meridian system. While working with a long-time patient who had an extreme phobia to water he tried a new idea. He got her to tap a meridian point under her eyes while she was fixating on her fear. Dr. Callahan had not expected the miracle that occurred during this session. His patient, who was simply tapping her face suddenly called out that her phobia was gone! She then proceeded to walk out to Dr. Callahan's pool and splash water from the pool onto her face. This had been the first time in two years that she had been able to even approach his pool, never mind touch the water. It truly appeared to be a miracle.

Callahan then took the necessary steps to develop this simple tapping technique into a recognized form of psychological treatment. He combined the "tapping" with simultaneous focusing on an issue. Callahan had discovered that if a person is focusing on a specific fear of their own at the time she taps, this fear could be removed, often permanently. He called this method *Thought Field Therapy* (TFT). Later, one of Callahan's students, Gary Craig, would simplify this method and define it as *Emotional Freedom Technique*, which he called "The One Minute Wonder".

Emotional Freedom Technique (EFT) or Tapping

The tapping technique works by releasing our trapped emotions and current overwhelming feelings. Often these feelings are layered upon each other – compiled of our unreleased emotions and traumas from previous experiences, often even unrelated to the current drama that is occurring; and these add up to make the current situation feel overwhelming.

When reactions are strongly triggered and we go into a full flight or fight response, tapping can be used to support us in the moment or used later when we have some private time to think back through what occurred and desensitize ourselves in a positive way, not running away from the feelings but fully empowering ourselves within the emotions of it and releasing anything that isn't serving us so that we are operating from "clean emotional energy." Results include reduced stress response, reduced negative emotion, reducing our ability to be retriggered and increasing our chances of remaining centered when thinking about or when involved in a future similar situation.

Both acupuncture and tapping work on the same principles. In fact I have created a chart on page 90, **The Power of the Tapping Points** - that lists the points and explores the potential emotional release that occurs when they are tapped. This is likened to the meridian points which are stimulated by acupuncturists and have been used by Chinese medical practitioners for thousands of years. Both draw the body's attention to an area that is blocked by agitating it a little bit and stimulating it. As the stimulation helps bring more blood flow to this particular area it helps clean it out so that it isn't clogged anymore and your electricity or energy can flow through your body unencumbered.

These areas become blocked, according to Chinese medicine, due to a number of reasons, one of them being unattended to emotions that we literally 'stuff' downwards into our body, resulting in a lack of energy flow. I have found, in my past, that unexpressed emotions have been very destructive to my life. They have created a number of different undesired experiences. These included feeling emotionally numb and depressed at one end of the scale to being angry and over-reactive in certain situations. When recovering from stress burnout I worked with a Chinese doctor and homeopath, who helped to heal much of my physical pain by supporting me to release trapped emotional issues – mostly anger and grief. At the time I didn't have this Tapping Tool to support myself. Now I find it invaluable to keep me emotionally supported and centered.

I particularly love it because, unlike acupuncture, tapping requires no equipment, only your fingers. Tap lightly, but firmly – imagine you are tapping someone on the shoulder to get his or her attention, that is the pressure you need apply. We use three fingers on a tapping point, which gives generous coverage, so you don't have to be exactly on the precious spot.

We can have physical responses repeat themselves with certain emotions, beliefs, and experiences. The power of **Tapping** is that we focus our mind, with a needle-like precision, on a very specific emotion and circumstance that is causing us distresses. We tap the specific points while we keep our minds focused on the stress-inducing situation and it unwinds our old past responses.

Tapping releases these feelings of being stressed and replaces them with feelings of being relaxed and grounded. It seems that our brains reset that association so that next time we have the same previously stressful experience our brain is going to remember, "Oh yes, I'm supposed to be calm now!" Then we are free to create new responses, one based on more rational beliefs and positive self-talk, which were covered in Chapter 8.

Tapping Explored

There are FOURTEEN tapping points in total; however, do not be concerned about getting them wrong or mixed up, the technique will still work even if you just tap on one spot. Still, using all points is the fastest way to release stuck emotions. I have also created a video to support you with this process and demonstrate the points and also a PDF diagram of the points. These can be found at www.ThriveNowToolkit.com.

The Tapping Session Set-Up

I offer a real live example on page 92, of how I apply this technique to support myself after my son has overwhelmed in a public place, but, in brief, a tapping session involves:

1. Explore and take note of the emotions involved in the situation.
2. Pick the most intense one to focus on to begin.
3. Gauge the intensity for yourself on scale of 0-10.
4. Start to Karate Chop your hands together while repeating the Set-Up Statement three (3) times.

Set-Up Statement

"Even though I feel . . .

_____

(add your most intense emotion here involved in problem)

. . . I still love honor and accept myself!"

Tapping Points In Order

Tapping points located on the body – tap each point approximately seven (7) times using three fingers for maximum coverage:

- **Karate Chop** – on the side of the hand about 1 inch down from the bottom of the little finger. This is the beginning point of all tapping sessions. Lightly tap the side of the hands while repeating the 'Set -Up Statement'

Then using three fingers, for maximum coverage tap while repeating most intense emotion:

- Top of head
- Eyebrow
- Outside of the Eye
- Under the Eye
- Under the Nose
- Chin
- Collarbone
- Rubbing from Under the Arm the bra line or mid chest for men.

Tapping points located on the Hand

- **Thumb** – outside base of the nail
- **Index Finger** – thumb side base of the nail
- **Middle Finger** – thumb side base of the nail
- **Little Finger** – thumb side base of the nail
- Back of Hand – known as the **Gamut Spot**, is located about 1 inch down from the knuckles in the indent between the ring finger and the little finger.

NOTE: AVOID TAPPING THE RING FINGER – but don't worry if you do by mistake nothing bad will happen!

The Power of the Tapping Points

Tapping Points	Negative Emotions When Blocked	When Released Increases
Karate Chop	Self-doubt, feeling vulnerable and lost, low confidence	Improves confidence, self-love, self-esteem, focuses direction
Top of Head	Scattered emotions	Balanced thoughts & feelings
Eyebrow	Trauma, fearful & inhibition	Courage
Side of Eye	Feel anger & resentment, depletes energy	Energy levels, determination & courage
Under Eye	Anxiety, phobias, loathing, unclear thinking	Sense of peace, clear thinking
Under Nose	Shyness, embarrassment	Confidence, enhances communication skills
Chin	Overwhelmed, shame, past emotional trauma	Emotional strength, energizes
Collarbone	Uncertainty, fear, tiredness	Creates drive & willpower to focus on tasks
Under Arm	Rejection, Low self-esteem, worried thoughts, envy	Ability to concentrate, confidence, speeds thinking & mental processing
Thumb	Grief, exhaustion	Vitality and positive thinking
Index Finger	Guilt, rigidity, stuck in past	Optimism, goal setting for positive future, Ability to be present in the NOW
Middle Finger	Instability, low self-esteem, disjointed thinking	Confidence building, self-worth, clarity & will-power
Little Finger	Loneliness, isolation, self-lessness and anger	Empathy, compassion, unconditional love
Gamut Spot	Blocked emotions, lack of love	Expressing emotions positively with others

Decoding My Triggered Emotions using Tapping

To make this more reality based and practical for you I decided to pick a real life scenario of my eldest son becoming aggressive, and overwhelming while in a public place. For me this is stressful as I think it probably is for most parents of children on the spectrum. This is not just a tool to support parents of children on the spectrum, it can be used for relationship challenges, feelings about self-esteem, anxiety, fears and anything that creates a negative emotional response within your world.

I worked with my husband, Paul Ward, who has studied Energetic Psychology and Tapping to support me while I worked through this scenario. I hope this will be easy for you to follow so you can understand how to work with this technique to support yourself and remember you always have the video to further guide your learning.

This is a real life example of being at our son's school, having everyone staring at us, other parents being surprised and shocked, some being irritated by the noise. Paul guided me to begin picturing this situation in my mind. I could feel my body respond to the scenario; it was running like a movie in my head.

The most powerful way to start working with tapping is to identify the leading emotions and feelings and write them down. Of course if you are out and about and need to access this tool don't stop yourself because you don't have a pen and paper in hand, just going through the tapping points, or as many as you can remember right there and then. Practicing tapping while actually in a stressful situation gets even faster results as you de-stress your body in the moment. However, in the beginning, taking the time to write down the feelings is an important part of the practice. Then the emotions need to be tackled one at a time. For me in the situation described, embarrassment is top of the list, so I begin here.

Working with Paul, I identified several thoughts and emotions involved in this scenario:
- Feeling embarrassed.
- Feeling judged by others.
- Feeling shame.
- Feeling helpless to stop my sons overwhelm in that moment.

- Feeling out of control of the situation because I had no support with me.
- Feeling scared that someone might call the police or security.
- Feeling angry with bystanders for their insensitive and unhelpful comments.
  (This has happened often to our family, people approach us saying such things as "Your child destroyed our meal"; "Can I talk to your child about his behavior; it's inappropriate"; "Is your child going to behave like that the whole time?")

Gauge Emotional Intensity

Having chosen **embarrassment** as my strongest emotion I then gauge the intensity of this feeling in the situation on a scale of 0-10, ten being the most intense. Once I have assigned a number, which in this situation was an 8 for me, I was able to begin. Later, I recheck my gauge of the emotional intensity of my embarrassment after completing a session focusing on this emotion.

Session Begins

To begin, I tap on my **karate chop** points, tapping my hands off each other and **repeat my Set-Up Statement (3) three times**. **"Even though I have this embarrassment about my son's melt down and overwhelm I still love, honor and accept myself."**

Note: If you find love, honoring and accepting yourself challenging right now, then you can also say "Even though I have this embarrassment about my son's melt down, I'm open to the idea that I can completely love, honor and accept myself". Most people, even if they don't feel like they are in total acceptance today, can imagine that one day they could be.

Next I start tapping the **crown of my head** and say "this embarrassment". And **inside of my eyebrow**, "this embarrassment". **Outside of my eye**, "I was so embarrassed, this embarrassment". **Under my nose** – "this embarrassment "– **under my chin** – "this embarrassment." And as I recall the details I begin adding them in here too while I tap my **collarbone** and move onto **under my arm** and say, "this embarrassment in the reception area of the school near the front door with the principal watching and parents there picking up their kids, while I'm watching my child in his blue Minecraft T-shirt, kicking and flailing on the floor. With everyone watching me in shock."

Then onto the **four finger points** and **gamut point** on front of the hand. "This embarrassment, as he screams and shouts and flails. This embarrassment."

Gauge Emotional Intensity Again

This finishes one round of all the points and I **take a deep breath** noticing how strong my feelings of embarrassment are now. And I notice that they are definitely reduced, gone down, from an 8 to a 4.

Repeat Tapping Session to Decrease Intensity Further

Ideally we want intensity to be at a zero, however sometimes that doesn't occur as the emotions are overlapping each other. So as we move through the session we may notice that the words begin to change and another layer of emotion begins to appear for example, being judged by others.

This emotion was second on my feeling list and is now ready to be explored. I double check where I am with the intensity of embarrassment making sure that it is at a zero or as close to as I can get right now. I have found that it usually only takes a few repetitions to release each emotion. Then I can begin to tackle the feeling of being judged.

I have discovered that sometimes my emotions are so strong that I can feel somewhat overwhelmed by them and they begin to get mixed up together. This can make it harder to take the edge off one of them when a series of emotions are fighting for attention all at the same time. In this case I take sometime to breathe, center myself with a mindfulness exercises—these are covered in the next section on page 95 and notice where my feet are. Then I roll my shoulders, yawn or sigh. This helps me let go before I begin, so I can be clearer about which emotion is actually the strongest. Then I begin there. As an Emotional Freedom Technique / Tapping practitioner once told me. "Imagine that you're in a forest full of trees and rather than slicing one tree at the bottom and then slicing the next tree at the bottom, you're taking a hedge clipper and topping the top inch off every single tree. It's going to take a lot longer before you even notice the trees being any shorter."

What we do with Tapping is, we chop down one tree at a time, and what we often see is that sometimes we may have 50 different trees, 50 different nuances of emotions and reactions and connections, and once we've chopped down a bunch of them, the whole thing topples. You don't always have to go through each and every one, once you've gotten the bulk of them the rest of them fall over as well and you're down to a 0 about the whole experience.

In summary, our stuck emotions and the blockages they cause can be cleared by Tapping, and we can remove these blockages, gently, slowly, one at a time thus clearing a pathway through our life, so that we can find that deeper sense of peace without being triggered by our past responses. Also, as you try this technique use words that are familiar to you, as your brain must make the connection between how you reacted in the past and how you are describing it now; only then can the neural pathways be cleared.

Tapping is the perfect tool to support those who have **anxiety**. If you are actually in a full-blown panic attack or overwhelm, then just gently tapping the points works to create relief in the moment. I have supported my son in this way many times, helping to de-energize his fear around certain circumstances that were overwhelming him.

You will find a PDF of the tapping points plus a video to support your learning at www.ThriveNowToolKit.com - Enjoy!

"Realize deeply that the present moment is all you have. Make the NOW the primary focus of your life."

Eckhart Tolle – The Power of Now:
A Guide to Spiritual Enlightenment

Mindfulness Meditation

The second Thrive Now tool for creating balance is **mindfulness meditation**. There are many types of meditation, and I cover other varieties in Chapter 14; however, mindfulness is the simplest form. Being mindful quickly helps you become more aware and balanced, increasing your energy and emotional balance in daily life.

The practice of mindfulness is a very ancient one. Although used in various religions such as Hinduism, Buddhism and Sikhism, it is not a religion. Mindfulness is a powerful tool for transformation, and using these techniques in no way conflicts with any religious doctrine of which I am aware. In fact mindfulness supports a deeper spiritual practice of whatever faith you are drawn to.

Mindfulness is simple. It is about being in the present moment. So simple, yet how much of your day do you actually spend in the here and now? It is not until you begin a conscious mindfulness practice that you realize how often you aren't actually allowing yourself to be in the now.

For example, have you ever driven somewhere and not remembered all the turns you made to reach your destination? Have you ever been in the check-out line and not remembered all the aisles you walked down or how everything got into your basket. You were working on automatic pilot. Your full awareness was not present in the moment, and you were mindlessly losing energy during your day.

Definition of mind-ful-ness

1. the quality or state of being conscious or aware of something. "their mindfulness of the wider cinematic tradition"

2. a mental state achieved by focusing one's awareness on the present moment, while calmly acknowledging and accepting one's feelings, thoughts, and bodily sensations, used as a therapeutic technique.

So in brief, all you need to do is bring your awareness to your present state. It is called a mindfulness practice because it is a 'practice,' not a 'perfection'. Often we think we are doing it wrong as our mind distracts us and our thoughts constantly pull us away to something in the future or past. However detach from getting it RIGHT and just chose to practice and have some fun with it. Personally when I began meditation I found it exceptionally hard. This is no longer the case and now I fit it in when and as often as I can.

I often do this while I drive to sharpen my brain and create a safer driving experience; however, don't start your practice here. Begin when you are at home or work in a quiet place and build your mindfulness muscles.

Follow these simple steps and apply them to your life anywhere you can. When my youngest son was in preschool his teacher would train the children in mindful walking as they went to lunch. This is a practical tool that increases your energy, stimulates your brain, decreases your stress levels and develops your self-awareness. It is totally free and only requires a few moments for you to reach success.

Research into mindfulness and special needs care workers is very telling, and suggests the impact that this practice can have on our own family as well as ourselves.

In 2009, The Journal of Applied Research in Intellectual Disabilities *2009*, (22, pp. 194-202*)* issued a report titled, **"Mindful Staff Can Reduce the Use of Physical Restraints When Providing Care to Individuals with Intellectual Disabilities**." (Singh 2009) This research followed twenty-three staff members in four group homes who participated in a twelve-week mindfulness meditation training program. The study ran for forty weeks. The researchers collected data on the number of aggressive incidents, staff injuries, peer injuries, staff verbal redirections and need to administer medication to reduce agitation. The results showed that during the forty weeks there were systematic decreases in incidents and that "the use of restraints and Stat medications decreased during mindfulness training and more substantially (to almost zero levels) during the mindfulness practice."

The conclusion from this study was that mindfulness **"provided the staff with a viable technology for changing their own behavior and the behavior of the individuals in their care."** It allowed the staff a way to focus on the current situation without necessarily drawing from the outcomes of past incidents with their clients. Being present reduced reactivity and judgment and decreased the staff's stress response.

I hope this study catches your attention and makes you think. This powerful and easy technique can change your life in many ways. Once you are comfortable with the technique you do not have to be in a calm place or isolated from others in order to practice. I practice these techniques often—in the car, at the store, waiting for appointments, walking my dog, even while I'm typing this line. The key is just becoming totally aware of your surroundings and how you are feeling at that very moment in time.

Your busy monkey mind will try to distract you often, but by just bringing your focus back to something in the present moment, like your foot on the floor, you instantly chose to be in the present and being there will begin to quiet your over busy mind.

Here is an example you can try while sitting; you can have your eyes open or closed:
- Take a deep breath in.
- Notice how you are feeling emotionally.
- Take another deep breath.
- Feel the seat of the chair beneath you.
- Feel your clothes touching the fabric of the chair and the firmness or softness of the backrest supporting you.
- Take a deep breathe bring your awareness to the air as it enters and leaves your nose or mouth.
- Notice how your body feels.
- Notice any sounds in your environment.
- Take another conscious breath.
- Feel the air as it enters your nose and follow it as it leaves your body on your exhale.
- Become aware of anything else that your body is feeling: cold or warmth, muscle tension, or relaxation.
- Be aware of your energy levels.
- Notice any thoughts you are having; don't attach, just be aware of them
- Continue your day being in the NOW!

As I tell my clients – this is the only moment that matters. You can't change the past and you can't predict the future. All you have is now and how you are being right now will allow your future to unfold with either ease and grace or pain and stress. You have the choice!

Weekly Goal:

Between NOW and this date: ___/___/___, I choose to try either tapping or mindfulness meditation to support my self-care.

(a) I chose Tapping as a way to release one situation that I find myself being emotionally triggered by. Describe this below:

_____

_____

_____

The most intense emotions that appear in that situation for me are:

_____

_____

_____

(b) Mindfulness Meditation Exercise. I chose to use this technique for ten minutes in my day for a week. Where I chose to try this and what results I experienced:

_____

_____

_____

Any "A-Ha!"s I received while practicing mindfulness.

_____

_____

_____

What benefits did I feel I received from achieving this goal?

_____

_____

_____

What negative outcome did I experience if not achieved?

_____

_____

_____

How I feel after achieving this goal ☺

_____

_____

_____

10

Sleeping with a Tiger in the Next Room

"Sleep is the golden chain that ties health and our bodies together."

Thomas Dekker author, 1570-1632

*W*hen we are suffering from excess stress in our lives, one of the first areas that can be affected is our sleep pattern. Children with autism, ADHD and Asperger's Syndrome often have disturbed sleep, and this can add to the stress cycle that affects our rest.

When my son was just two I gave him an over-the-counter cold medication recommended by his doctor. The result was horrifying. My son became completely hyperactive, throwing himself against the wall for hours and then jumping on my bed from midnight until five in the morning. He was manic, and there seemed to be no off button. When he finally fell asleep around dawn, I was beyond tired. Reading the microscopic small print on the label I saw later that it advised, "May cause excitability in some children." If I'd only been able to bottle that energy I would be a millionaire. Now when my son gets his late night energy, we support him with a low dose of melatonin that instantly works to calm his system and send him into a restful night's sleep. However, after supporting many parents, I know that sleep challenges aren't unusual. One of the moms I interviewed, Nancy Battye, speaks of surviving on four hours of broken sleep a night while her two daughters with cerebral palsy were growing up. They needed constant intervention at night and regular emergency hospital visits. She even slept with her shoes on ready to jump into action when needed. Nancy also speaks in Chapter 13 about how this sleep deprivation eventual took a major toll on her health and ability to focus.

Sleep is extremely important. During sleep time our body undergoes repair and detoxification. While we sleep the body rests, our immune system re-boosts itself, and our brain processes our day during dreamtime. Poor sleep patterns are linked to poor health. Those who sleep less than six hours a night have a shorter life expectancy than those who sleep for longer. Lack of sleep affects your ability to think and react appropriately in situations. It lowers your sex drive, increases the risk of accidents when driving, and can add to the symptoms of depression. Sleeplessness can age your skin and make you gain weight, for lack of sleep as been shown to increase appetite and even hunger levels. And if all that was not enough research published (Whitehall II (also known as the Stress & Health Study) 2007) in England in 2007 indicated that lack of sleep doubled the risk of death from cardiovascular disease. So sleep has a profound effect on our mental, emotional and physical well-being.

When I was suffering from chronic fatigue, I could do nothing but sleep. Yet the sleep wasn't restful; I awoke as exhausted as when I went to bed. Sometimes I didn't make it to my bed and would nod off while eating or watching TV or at a movie. This was debilitating. I have also experienced other times in my life when I couldn't find sleep. I was tossing and turning, waking often during the night and this was equally frustrating. Both conditions reduced my quality of life.

During my journey to heal my body, I studied the nature of sleep and what was necessary for a healthy sleep pattern. I became familiar with the natural flow of our body called circadian rhythms. I became aware that sleep and the correct amount of sun light were crucial to deep restful sleep. I learned the ways in which diet and certain aspects of our home environment could support sleep and the ways in which stress impacts our sleep cycles.

I discovered what factors affect our sleep in negative and positive ways. Some of my findings are not that well publicized; some may seem like "old wives tales." Yet all the techniques are easy to implement and have worked for myself and my clients over the years.

The first area I looked at when it came to sleep was diet.

Foods that stop us from sleeping like a baby

- Caffeine after 6 in the evening
- Heavily spiced foods
- Overly large meals
- Fatty foods
- Sugary snacks
- Excessive alcohol

These foods either stimulate an excess of adrenaline in the system, as sugar and caffeine do, or they disturb our digestion. Although we may find it easy to drift off to sleep, the quality of sleep is usually affected because the body has to work harder to digest and metabolize the food instead of focusing on the task of replenishing the body.

Foods that help us sleep and why

The body needs the right amount of melatonin and serotonin for a relaxed night's sleep. Melatonin is produced from the correct amount of natural sunlight which I will talk more about in the next section. Serotonin is the feel good, relaxing hormone that is chemically produced by many anti-depressants such a Prozac.

Also linked to the production of serotonin through a series of chemical reactions is tryptophan an essential amino acid, which means your body can't manufacture it. Foods that help this reaction contain either the right amount of complex-carbohydrate or tryptophan itself.

The right amount of complex–carbohydrate stimulates the body to release tryptophan into the bloodstream, while serotonin is synthesized and this helps the body feel sleepy.
Foods such as:
- half of a baked potato,
- slice of whole grain toast,
- whole grain crackers,
- glass of warm milk (yes grandma was right!).

Foods containing tryptophan
- turkey
- chicken
- pork
- cheese

Color

Psychologists agree that color affects our mood, emotion and even behavior. Many ancient civilizations used color as part of their healing practices. In the National Institute of Health in Washington DC, researchers discovered the effect that different light has on living cells. They found that blue made the cells expand and move away from each other, red contracted them and green light actually killed them (green is a very relaxing color to wear, just not as a light). Other research has found color effective in helping Parkinson's Disease, discovering that wearing green lenses diminished tremors as it acted to cut out the red and yellow rays in daylight, both of which are activators.

I studied color therapy many years ago in Ireland and have found it effective in helping to reduce stress in my clients as it can create relaxation on many levels – mind, body and spirit.

Often our sleep gets disturbed when we are experiencing chronic stress. As parents of ultra-sensitive special needs kids who are often poor sleepers, our sleep can be diminished if, during the night, we need to look after a hyper child or a child with health issues. What I will outline to help you sleep better is also applicable to your children.

In a psychological test performed in the UK, four equal sized rooms were painted different colors: yellow, red, blue and green. Video cameras were installed in each one. A seat and journal was provided to each participant. The participants were asked to record their feelings during the time spent in each room. The results were interesting and illustrate how color can impact our sleep.

The yellow room made participants feel happy and energized, yet they also felt like they wanted to write on the wall and not in the book provided. People moved through this room pretty quickly, not really wanting to sit for long. There was a lot of conversation in this room.

People also moved through the red room quickly, not sitting for long. They also used more body movements as they went through it. Feelings recorded ranged from warm and energized to angry.

In the blue room, people sat for longer periods, relaxing, with their bodies obviously less agitated than when they were in the red room. Little conversation occurred. The feelings recorded ranged from relaxed, mellow, content, to sad and cold.

The green room reminded people of nature. They felt expanded and relaxed here also. They felt their breathing deepen. Feelings were content, relaxed, though some felt nauseous.

I have personally experimented with different colored bed linens to see if I was affected or not. I have found that my worst sleep occurred in yellow, orange and red sheets. Those colors were great to increase the passion in your relationship and for romance, but not so good for sleep! Blues, green, light pinks, lavenders all resulted in a better night's sleep. This also extends to the color of the pajamas, walls and flooring. Be mindful of these reactions, and try to incorporate more relaxing colors for you and your children; it will improve everyone's sleep.

Sound

Many of us have sensitive hearing, so wearing earplugs or having a white noise machine in your room can be helpful to block out unwanted background noise. Try playing relaxing music or use a guided visualization to relax the nervous system before bedtime. Avoid the sounds of water flowing at bed time for obvious reasons.

Media Diet

Watching the news or reading negative newspaper reports before bed also adds to our stress and anxiety, which makes it more difficult to find a restful natural sleep. I put myself on a news fast almost eighteen years ago and haven't missed out on anything yet. If a report is important for me to read, I will find out about it on MSN.com or some social media platform. I have also found that my children become more agitated when the news is on in our house. They pick-up on the drama and negative stories and start to act out by fighting or overwhelming.

You might also consider the types of books you read before bed. Try to make sure they offer inspiration and relaxation instead of adrenaline rushes and extreme violence.

Sunlight and sleep

All human beings need natural full spectrum light for optimum health, as it is essential for our well-being. It supports physical vitality, vision health, and mineral absorption. Unfortunately for many of us, we work indoors and even our children spend many hours indoors under unnatural lighting. Getting natural sunlight everyday helps improve sleep and has a positive effect on our brain chemistry.

Lack of sunlight has been linked with Seasonal Affective Disorder (SAD) and depression. Some of the symptoms of light starvation are irritability, fatigue, lowered immune defenses, insomnia, overeating, and depression. This is more prevalent in countries that have long dark winters.

However, it is thought that SAD wintertime depression affects some ten million Americans each year. Research shows that those living in sunnier places such as Florida have a much lower rate of SAD then those living in New York where winters are longer and darker. If we look outside of America, a link has been suggested between the high suicide rate in Scandinavia and its long dark winters.

There are two main types of lighting in buildings,- incandescent bulbs (household bulbs) and fluorescent bulbs. Neither of these contains the same range of colors as natural light. Incandescent bulbs are deficient in the blue end of the spectrum, and contain virtually no ultra violet light. They emit much of their output as yellow and red. The visual effects of this can be seen in an indoor photograph: when a flash fails to work, everyone looks slightly jaundiced.

Fluorescent bulbs produce a distorted spectrum of light that is deficient in the areas of the red and blue-violet rays, and is strongest in the orange, yellow and green end of the spectrum. Orange and yellow are activating colors that energize the body and stimulate the brain while green helps to bring balance. The blue, and violet colors help relax and heal the body, thus extended periods of exposure to fluorescent lighting can over stimulate, as suggested in 1980 by Dr. Fritz Hollwich of Germany. (Fritz Hollwich 1980)

Hollwich conducted a study on the effects of sitting under fluorescent lighting compared to full spectrum lighting, i.e. sunshine. Using blood tests, his study observed changes in the endocrine system of people under the different lighting systems. The results were dramatic. He noted that those under the fluorescent lighting had higher levels of stress hormones in their blood; both ACTH (adrenocorticotrophic hormone) and Cortisol were discovered. In contrast, when tested, those sitting outdoors had no such hormones. This study resulted in cool-white fluorescent lighting being made illegal in German hospitals and medical facilities. Yet millions of us spend most of our days in facilities sitting under such lights.

So what does it mean to have ACTH and Cortisol in the blood stream? We have already discussed the "flight or fight" response in depth, that series of biochemical changes that help us deal with perceived threat or danger. That response gives us the extra energy needed to get away from the Saber Toothed Tiger that was once a threat to our primitive predecessors.

When in a state of stress, the immune system is suppressed; the digestive system shuts down; heart rate, breathing rate, muscle tension, metabolism and blood pressure all increase. Adrenaline levels increase in the body. Blood is pumped from hands, feet and digestive organs to the large muscles of the legs and arms to assist in the fight or flight.

This stress response can be useful as it gives us extra energy to get a job done quickly or finish a project on time; however, a problem occurs when this response is ongoing and the body does not have a chance to release the adrenaline and return the body to a relaxation response.

When this happens, the immune system becomes suppressed for long periods of time, the digestive system is struggling to work, the muscles are tense, and the unreleased adrenaline makes it hard to sit still and concentrate. So you can see the effect this may have on people who spend a large amount of time under fluorescent lighting, particularly if they are already suffering from stress in their lives.

Light affects the body both physically and vibrationally. Physically, light reaches the eyes through the optic nerves. From the optic nerves, light then travels to the brain into the hypothalamus and then to the pineal gland. The hypothalamus is the main switch for the stress response located within the mid-brain, while the pineal gland is a small gland that helps to regulate the hormonal, and neurochemical functioning of the whole body.

It is in charge of releasing a chemical called 'Melatonin' also known as the **sleep hormone**. Melatonin is involved in naturally bringing the body to a state of rest. The balancing of our hormonal system is essential to good vitality levels and brain functioning. As a result, light plays a role in the overall health of our physical body, emotional well-being, and sleep patterns.

Light is composed of waves of radiant energy, measured in wavelength. Wavelength is determined by the distance between consecutive wave crests, which is measured in nanometers. Visible light ranges from 400 to 700 nanometers in wavelength. Full spectrum light contains the seven visible colors of the light spectrum: Red, Orange, Yellow, Green, Blue, and Violet. We can see these lights when we look at a rainbow or at light shining through a prism. Natural sunlight also contains ultra-violet light, associated with tanning, and infrared light, associated with heating. However, neither is visible to the human eye.

I notice how my body becomes stressed and my brain begins to struggle when I spend more than thirty minutes under fluorescent lighting. I feel this form of lighting may be a huge problem for most of us and probably even more so for our children. I also feel that it may be impacting their behavior and functioning within the classroom and affecting their ability to get a deep restful sleep later in the day.

So what can we do to help ourselves stay more balanced in regards to light?

- **An hour of natural light** a day, keeps the doctor away. Being outdoors during the morning time or late afternoon when the intensity of the sunlight is decreased is said to be beneficial for the body. It is best to remove eyeglasses or sunglasses and allow your body to absorb the healing rays of the sun. However, do not look directly at the sun, but try sitting in the shade where light can still enter the eyes. Also, be cautious that your child's sensitive skin doesn't burn.

- Take outdoor **daily physical activity**: Exercise is essential for the body to stay physically and neurochemically healthy. Exercise helps to burn off the stress hormones that have built up in the body, rebalancing the sympathetic nervous system, which controls our stress responses. Exercising in daylight also lets the body absorb vital natural light that is essential to health.

- Sunlight is also essential for **Vitamin D** production, which I talk about later in the chapter on nutrition, but in brief, Vitamin D prevents osteoporosis, depression, prostate cancer, breast cancer, and even affects diabetes and obesity.

- Eat **fresh natural produce**: Fresh produce grown under natural sunlight will have higher nutritional value than processed foods.

- Have **full spectrum bulbs** in your work area and throughout your own home. These can be bought relatively cheaply and are available globally. When I lived in Ireland, I had a full spectrum light box that I used during my office hours. I found it kept my energy levels high even when working on the computer.

- **Replace fluorescent** bulbs and incandescent bulbs with full spectrum alternatives. This is the ideal, but perhaps not always practical, especially in large public schools.

The power of aromatherapy oils

Lavender, rose oil, and ylang ylang all relax the nervous system. I often put one drop on my son's pillow to help him sleep or add it to our baths in the evenings.

Technology

Most people do not realize that our standard bedside clock-radio can have a negative effect on sleep patterns. Believe it or not, if it is plugged into the wall, it then emanates a frequency. While this is not disruptive in itself, it is disruptive to your immune system as it attempts to recharge. I know this might sound bizarre, but trust me when I tell you, electricity around our bed is not a good thing. Televisions, Wi-Fi, clock radios, computers and other such technology affect us when we sleep. When I first learnt about this, over eighteen years ago, I instantly went to visit my Nana. She was in her late seventies and was a total insomniac for years. I asked her to try unplugging her clock radio and electric blanket while she slept and to do this for a week and see if it made a difference to her sleep. My Nana lived in Raheny village, in a one-hundred-year-old cottage that was cold even in the summer. I told her not to worry, she could warm her bed and then unplug the blanket just before she got into bed. I knew she didn't keep it turned on while she slept.

My Nana was quite a skeptical old lady, but she agreed to TRY IT for the week. I'm sure she agreed just to humor me, her eldest granddaughter. Anyway, after the week elapsed, she never plugged the radio or blanket in again, because her sleep patterns were so improved. She even started to tell all her friends this little known secret.

Another secret I always share with my clients is to use baking soda or bread soda around electricity. I place it in small tubs under the beds and change it every 6–8 weeks. It soaks up the smells in our fridges but it also soaks up extra electricity in our air. Be cautious with this, as it is poisonous, so keep it out of reach of small children who like to taste everything. When I worked as a desk-top publisher I was surrounded with technology all day. I got the nickname "cocaine kid" as I had tubs of baking soda all around my desk. However the day I forgot the baking soda, I really could feel the difference in my energy levels. I felt drained and put upon.

Over the last sixteen years, I have been sharing these insights at all my workshops and have heard amazing results from this cheap alternative for boosting and maintaining energy levels.

Electromagnetic Stress

If you live very close to a large electrical tower or big generator, this can affect your immune system and can also create excessive anger. At one of my workshops a women brought a photo of her children and asked me if I could give her some advice to help them. I looked at the photos and instantly felt electricity and anger without any promoting from her. I asked her did she have an electrical tower, or pylon, as we call them in Ireland, close to her house. She paled and explained that there was one in her front yard, she could hear it buzzing at night, it was so close. I shared my knowledge about the damage excess electricity can have on the human body. Our bodies vibrate at a particular rate that is not in harmony with electricity. There are now a number of products on the market that help clear your properties or place of work from electromagnetic stress.

Summary

Here are eleven tips to help you have a better night's sleep and increase your well-being.

1. **Drink warm milk before bed**; this releases serotonin, a feel good chemical, into your body, which helps you relax. Chamomile tea is also a good to aid relaxation.

2. A **warm bath** before bedtime will help relax your muscular system and quiet your mind. Adding Epsom salts to the water can help to relieve muscular pain. You could also add a few drops of lavender oil to your bath water to increase the relaxation effect, or put a couple of drops on the underside of your pillow to aid sleep. (Always read the label of any aromatherapy oil carefully and get professional advice before using, particularly if you are taking medication, pregnant or suffering from illness.)

3. **Practicing deep abdominal breathing** coming up to bedtime and while in bed will greatly reduce stress and anxiety in body and assist with sleep.

4. **Avoid the consumption of caffeine** after 6.00 o'clock in the evening. Caffeine increases the stress response in the body and gives you an adrenaline rush.

5. **Reduce your sugar** and refined carbohydrate intake before bedtime. Too much sugar in your body will give you excess energy, making it difficult to unwind.

6. **Regular exercise** during your day, for 20 minutes, will help reduce stress built up in your body and help regulate your body's metabolism, thus assisting with sleep. Vigorous exercise prior to bedtime is not recommended as this can increase your energy buzz.

7. **Journaling to express your emotions** has been shown to reduce stress chemicals in the body and increase the relaxation response. You can also visualize a box outside your door into which you can imagine putting all your problems and any voice that might be still be whirling around in your head.

8. **Get a massage**. One-hour of massage is equal to three or four hours of sleep. It relaxes your whole body, mind and spirit.

9. **Practice Progressive Muscular Relaxation** - tightening and relaxing different muscle groups in your body while working with deep abdominal breathing. This can be done throughout your day, but is also excellent while in bed to relax the body and mind. We cover this in more detail in Chapter 12.

10. Be **cautious of electrical equipment** plugged in around your bed while you sleep, such as an electrical blanket, cell phone, clock-radio, etc. Electrical charges around your bed at night make it more difficult for your immune system to recharge itself as it is constantly working to stop your body from absorbing the electromagnetic stress during the night.

11. Take a supplement especially designed to support deep sleep. One that contains a low dosage of **melatonin** can work well but get advice from your medical doctor if you have concerns or are taking other medication.

Weekly Goal:

Between NOW and this date: ___/___/___ , I choose to support myself getting the best sleep possible by making these simple changes:

_____
_____
_____
_____

Benefit to achieving this goal

_____
_____
_____
_____

Negative outcome if not achieved

_____
_____
_____
_____

How I feel after achieving this goal ☺

_____
_____
_____
_____

11

Diet and Nutrition

*"We are indeed much more than what we eat,
but what we eat can nevertheless help us
to be much more than what we are."*
Alice May Brock – author, artist, and restaurateur.

Seeing the effect that food has on my children was one of my greatest learning curves. My beloved son Oisin, in the space of six months, went from being a typical child with high functioning autism to being a highly aggressive, volatile and sometimes dangerous individual. It took working with a very knowledgeable biomedical specialist, Doctor Geoffrey Radoff, founder of Trinity Alternative Medical Care, to figure out what had made that shift happen. The change was primarily due to his diet.

My older son was already on a gluten free and mostly organic diet, but more needed to be adjusted. He had developed an extremely high re-activity to sugar and so the gluten free chocolate chip cookies I was putting in his lunch box for treats were no longer a suitable option. They had become deadly! This dramatic situation, where we almost had to hospitalize him due to his extreme behavior, made me review once more all I knew about nutrition and the truly important part it plays in our overall health and emotional well-being.

What I will discuss in this chapter is nutrition in relationship to stress. There are many diets you can follow to increase your health and well-being and I am not here to tell you to eat a particular way. What I do wish to share with you is the importance of the vitamins we absorb and how these can impact our emotional and physical response both for our children as well as ourselves. I also want to bring your awareness to foods that can create increased stress responses in our body.

I have created a **Complimentary Power-Up Your Nutrition Blueprint**, also available for download at www.ThriveNowToolkit.com.

Although this chapter may contain a good deal of information you already know, it is still worthwhile reviewing. Just knowing does not mean we always do that which is most important to keep us healthy. After I had suffered from stress burnout, I realized I needed to adjust much of what I ate. I needed to stabilize my blood sugars and wean myself off the extreme amount of caffeine I was consuming with my 6-8 cups a day.

Complex Carbohydrates are key

If we remember back to biology or home economics classes, carbohydrates make up the greater part of our diet and are obtained from grains, fruit, vegetables, legumes, nuts and most processed foods.

Complex carbohydrates (fruit, vegetables and whole-grains) are the best way to obtain these, as they come complete with nutrients and act somewhat like a time-release capsule.

Refined carbohydrates such as simple sugars flood the body with sugar as soon as they are absorbed. Although this supplies the body with quick flashes of energy, it is a false high, followed by a long period of lethargy.

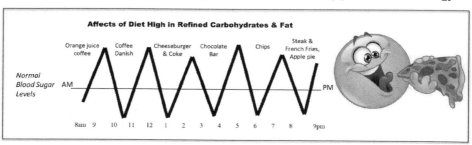

The complex carbohydrate in comparison **slowly releases sugar** so helping to maintain blood sugar levels within your body. This is essential to manage stress as the body needs more energy when coping with a stressful situation and requires constant blood sugar. (See diagram below)

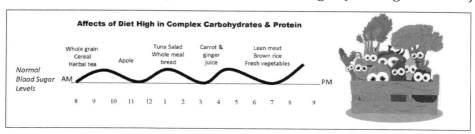

Watching what you drink

"Water is the most neglected nutrient in your diet, but one of the most vital"

Julia Child, American chef, author, and television personality.

We all consume drinks during our day. Everywhere we go we see a coffee store on the corner inviting us in. Taking a break here is aligned with creating a *Thrive Now Blueprint*, particularly if you chose to journal and explore the exercises in this book while you sip your herbal tea or cup of coffee. When I was growing up in Ireland there was always a pot of tea brewing should anyone call. It is an essential part of many of our social and cultural interactions: chat over a cup of coffee, go for a beer with friends; open a bottle of wine at the end of a day; stand around the water cooler at work. Yet what we drink in our day can impact our stress levels positively or negatively.

In March 2013 the US Beverage Digest reported a dramatic change in the American diet. Soda, which had been number one for many years as beverage of choice, has now been superseded by water. That means the average amount of water people drink has increased 38 percent to about 58 gallons a year. Bottled water has led that growth, with consumption nearly doubling to 21 gallons a year. So I know I am already speaking to the converted, however I just wanted to share with you why water is so important for our bodies.

First, water plays an integral part in the healthy functioning of the human body. The average adult body contains about 80 pints of water. 60-65% of a man's body comprises water and 50-60% of a woman's. It is also essential to the success of any weight loss or exercise program. Drinking 1.5 liters of mineral or filtered water a day is your best option. If you can, *avoid* water that is *chlorinated or carbonated.*

Other drinks such as teas, sodas and coffee don't count towards our water intake. In fact drinks containing caffeine act as a mild diuretic - that is, it makes you urinate more than you would without it.

Over consumption of drinks such as soda, black tea and coffee create acid in the system. Excess acid adds to the stress response in the body, creating digestive challenges, heartburn and often increased irritability. It's this

irritability which I have found leaves me vulnerable to increased stress during my son's challenging behaviors. However one or two cups of coffee or black or green tea a day can be beneficial.
(I offer more details on caffeine in my Power-Up Nutrition Blueprint)

As a nation our awareness of the relationship between health and nutrition has increased. Television shows like "The Biggest Loser," "Dr. Oz", and "Jamie Oliver Food Revolution," to name but a few, are all encouraging us to look at our daily food intake. However we still have a way to go when we look at how many hamburgers McDonald's sells in a day in the United States—approximately 4.2 million.

When I burnt out from stress I quickly realized that my basic foundation in nutrition was misaligned. I didn't have a foundation of health to build a balanced life upon. Increasing my fresh fruit and vegetable intake, decreasing my caffeine, drinking more water, eating leaner protein and improving my carbohydrate intake were all a great start to strengthening my immune system and reducing my stress responses. I'm not telling you to throw out your chocolate chip cookies! Don't try to make all these changes at once – I'm not trying to ADD stress to your day! Strive for a little change, day by day, while noticing improvements in your energy.

To further improve my health I also needed to look at my vitamin levels.

Vitamins for Optimum Health

"Those who think they have no time for healthy eating will sooner or later have to find time for illness."
Edward Stanley (1826-1893), from The Conduct of Life

Vitamins and minerals are necessary for our health and well-being. When I began working with a stress management coach as part of my stress-burnout recovery, one of the first things she told me was that my body needed the right balance of vitamins and minerals, especially when I was under pressure and living an extremely busy life. Vitamins and minerals were especially important as my body used up its resources at a much faster pace when in extreme stress.

Ideally, we can get the right balance of essential vitamins and minerals from our food; however, often what we consume has been artificially modified and chemically sprayed, thus reducing its goodness.

According to nutritional expert Dr Andrew Weil author of Spontaneous Happiness: *"Micronutrient deficiencies are common in our population. I am on record as saying that dietary supplements are not substitutes for good diets, but they are good insurance against gaps in the diet. I grow a lot of my own food, prepare it myself, and am thoughtful about what I eat. I also take a good daily multivitamin/multimineral supplement and advise you to do so too, because I consider it another good and safe measure to optimize emotional and physical well-being."*

If you do chose to take vitamins, a good quality multivitamin is probably your best option. Try to find living or whole food ones. These have been minimally processed which allows maximum absorption within the body. Taking vitamins is not a replacement for healthy eating and never should be, but a balance of both healthy eating and vitamins will greatly increase your body's healing capacity.

VERY IMPORTANT: Remember that your digestive system shuts down when you are in a flight or fight response, so being mindful of how you feel when you take your supplements is also important. If you feel excessively stressed or have just dealt with an overwhelming situation then nothing you eat will be absorbed into the body because the body turns off the digestive system and pumps blood from this area into the large muscles of the legs and arms to give you more speed to fight or escape. Ideally you should take ten minutes to create a relaxation response in the body with deep abdominal breathing, some progressive muscular relaxation, or mindfulness meditation to reduce the stress response and benefit the most from what you are consuming.

Here is a list of the ESSENTIAL VITAMINS & MINERALS FOR OPTIMUM HEALTH

- **Vitamin A** is essential for growth.

- **Vitamin B complex** is essential when under stress, supports reduction of anxiety and decreased mood swings.

- **Vitamin B-12** is essential for growth, development and energy.

- **Vitamin C** is a super charged vitamin, essential to heal our body from stress and boost our immune system also one we need to absorb daily as your body doesn't store it or make it.

- **Vitamin D** strong heart and mind.

- **Vitamin E** is essential for normal antibody responses.

- **Calcium** promotes strong bones and muscles.

- **Essential Fatty Acids- ALA, DHA, EPA** which refers to their chemically structure, are not made in the body, you need to get them from your diet. Omega 3, 6 and 9, are fatty acids that are required for optimum health – optimum brain function and increased concentration, increased emotional balance, maintains stamina, supports healthy weight levels and more.

- **Iron** is a mineral and functions primarily as a carrier of oxygen in the body, essential for increased energy levels.

- **Magnesium** prevents disease and assists in stress management. It coats the nerves and assists in the absorption of calcium.

- **Potassium** is a key essential vitamin that lowers blood pressure.

In my **Power-Up Nutrition Blueprint** I present in-depth details about all the above vitamins and outline **which foods are rich in them**. I also explore other areas of diet that are essential to your health and well being. I hope you enjoy this!

Weekly Goal:

Between NOW and this date: ___/___/___, I choose to give myself the greatest chance to Thrive by incorporating new vitamins or adjusting my nutrition in this way:

_____

_____

_____

_____

Benefit to achieving this goal

_____

_____

_____

_____

Negative outcome if not achieved

_____

_____

_____

_____

How I feel after achieving this goal ☺

_____

_____

_____

_____

12

Your Thrive Now Blueprint

**"Happiness is not something ready made.
It comes from your own actions."**
His Holiness the 14th Dalai Lama (1935- present)

My greatest challenge is handling my son at times of aggressive overwhelms. I have come to understand many of his triggers, however, and have created a system that helps me avoid those as much as possible. Some of those triggers and my solutions for avoiding them might help you. For sudden loud noises, I have noise canceling headphones on hand and in my car when needed. To deal with adventures or sudden changes, no matter how fun, I need to constantly 'front load', a term I garnered from our first occupational therapist.

Many of you may already be familiar with this term 'front load', it means informing him in as much detail as possible what will occur the next day. Often we use Google to study where we might go before we go there. For example when we chose to go to Legoland for the first time, we studied the Legoland site in detail. Looking at what was available to eat, where the restrooms where, what rides he might like to try, where to meet me if he got lost and what he could do to regulate himself if he became over whelmed or scared.

Depending on the size of the adventure we begin this up to a week or more in advance. For more routine trips to places like the movies or restaurant we still study everything online, watch the trailers, read the menu etc. Often if it is convenient and an important meal out, I visit the restaurant before we go to check gluten free and sugar free options, check for noise levels, talk to staff and judge their comfort level with a child that will probably want to run up and down at some point, book the perfect table away from the crowd etc. Then the day of, I repeat to him what is going to happen and talk about expectations and again go through his self-calming options. He has chosen some that really support him, such as having pictures of his therapy guinea pig on his phone to look at, wearing his favorite my little pony t-shirt or hat, having some homeopathic rescue remedy gum or pastels in his pocket for anxious moments, and carrying headphones to listen to his favorite music on his phone. Creating independence is our biggest goal with him. The more empowered he feels to support himself, the calmer he is.

To avoid high amounts of sugar, I always have lean turkey meat to give him before any sugary snacks to counterbalance blood sugar rush. To avoid lack of food, I include regular snacks every 3-4 hours such as low fat cheese stick or a hand full of nuts. If his technology breaks down or we are going somewhere he can't bring his computer, I have apps on my phone – and pictures of guinea pigs that particularly soothe him.

Normally I receive all this energy when an overwhelm does occur because I am the main caregiver and my husband travels frequently. Often I've been bitten, pushed, pinched or body slammed or have to gently restrain him as he has a habit of hitting himself in the head with objects when very upset. This can be exhausting on all levels.

Having a two-year old with a temper tantrum is one thing, but dealing with a one hundred thirty pound, 5-foot, 8-inch twelve year old is a very different ball game. The more balanced I can stay in this situation, the shorter is the time that my son overwhelms. If I become reactive all is usually lost for at least an hour sometimes up to 4 hours. I'm sure many of you reading this will know what I mean. However, for me to be able to remain in that less reactive state requires a good deal of conscious self-care. In this chapter I will cover some of the ways I have found that really support me in having a deeper relaxation response in my day.

Just as illness is often brought about by the accumulation of many little tensions, so can wellness be brought about by the practice of little relaxations, which you will have seen if you previously downloaded my **Complimentary Thrive Now Mini Book** at my website **www.SiobhanWilcox.com**. One of the simplest ways of dealing with stress is to interrupt the accumulation of stress by taking breaks during the day to discharge tension. It is important to try and find at least a few techniques that you can use anywhere at anytime. Try to use them regularly, at least a few times a day, preferably before the aches and pains creep in, but definitely at the first sign of tension or pain. At first it might seem a little awkward to take these breaks; however once you practice them a few times it starts to feel as simple as the "That Was Easy" Button from Staples.

One Minute Stress Busting Miracle Tools

1a. Body Focus - Take a deep breath and close your eyes for a few moments. Sense where your body is contacting the environment around you (chair, floor, etc.), sense where your weight is resting. Now take another deep breath and move your body in some way to get more comfortable and relaxed.

1b. Same as above but sense if there are any places of excess tension or pain in the body. If you find one, take a deep breath and try to imagine that place loosening up. Then gently and slowly move that part of the body just a little bit to let it loosen and relax.

2. Creative breathing (make sure the belly goes out as you inhale – babies have it right!)

2a. Take a slow deep breath in through the nose and out through the mouth.

2b. Breathe in through the nose and out through the mouth to the following count.

1-2-3-4,	1-2-3-4,	1-2-3-4
Inhale	hold	exhale

Pause before the next breath

2c. Same as the beginning of above but exhaling for longer

1-2-3-4,	1-2-3-4,	1-2-3-4-5-6-7-8
Inhale	hold	exhale slowly,

Pause before the next breath

3. **Yawning**

   Breathe in and out through the mouth and roll your tongue back to the roof of your mouth and move it sideways along the soft palate until you start to yawn. Then open your mouth as wide as it will go, breathe in and let yourself yawn as long as you can.

4. **Neck stretches**

   Gently let your head stretch to the left, then to the right, then down to your chest. Then slowly circle around in one direction, then circle back around in the other direction. Don't stretch your head in the backwards direction as it may strain the vertebrae. Always be gentle on your neck as it is sensitive to being strained.

5. **Shoulder rolls**

   With your hands in your lap, firmly but slowly circle the shoulders around as far as they will go. Do this a few times, then relax and finish by shrugging a few times. You can also try one shoulder at a time and try different speeds as well.

6. **Body clapping**

   Using the palms and fingers or lightly clenched fists start gently slapping every inch of your body. Be gentle on tender areas and firm on the rest. Start at the ankles and work upwards.

Developing Your Own Personal Thrive Now Blueprint – what are your favorites

Immediate Thrive Strategies

- ☐ Laughter
- ☐ Get or Give a Hug
- ☐ Rational Thinking – Chapter 8
- ☐ Mindfulness Meditation – Chapter 9
- ☐ Emotional Freedom Technique – TAPPING – Chapter 9
- ☐ Chose a One Minute Stress Busting Miracle Tools – see page 123

Short-term Thrive Strategies

- ☐ Journaling
- ☐ Get a Massage
- ☐ Moderate Exercise
- ☐ Soak in a Soothing Bath
- ☐ Progressive Muscular Relaxation – described on page 128
- ☐ Talk about Problems – Join our Online Thrive Training
- ☐ Visualization see Chapter 6 and page 130 for more details
- ☐ Connect on our Facebook Group & get a Virtual Hug plus Support
- ☐ Practice some Gentle Yoga Poses
- ☐ Take a Break in Nature to Re-balance Your Energy – Yes you can even HUG a TREE!

Long-term Thrive Strategies

- ☐ Regular Yoga Practice
- ☐ Supportive Friendships
- ☐ Daily Gratitude Practice
- ☐ Regular Aerobic Exercise
- ☐ Continue to Study and Learn
- ☐ Spiritual Practice – Chapter 14
- ☐ Lifelong Commitment to Self-Care
- ☐ Daily Practice of Self-Love & Compassion
- ☐ Practice Positive Affirmations
- ☐ Set Yourself Goals that are FUN to Achieve
- ☐ Integration of Rational Self Talk – Chapter 8
- ☐ Regular Relaxation Techniques – see page 127
- ☐ Hire a Coach for Support and Continuous Growth
- ☐ Healthy Diet – Chapter 11 and Download the Power-Up Nutrition Blueprint
- ☐ Find things that inspire and elevate you in your day – start by signing up for my Complimentary Quote in Action at my website www.SiobhanWilcox.com
- ☐ Find a way to GIVE BACK and make a difference. My boys and I regularly volunteer. Sometimes we feed the homeless (my son loves to bag groceries), or clean the local beach, weed at the schools community garden. Giving back feeds our souls.

Relaxation Thrive Now Tools

Meditation Techniques

Mindfulness Meditation – Covered in Chapter 9

Breathing techniques

Creative Breathing – page 123 in **One Minute Stress Busting Miracle Tools**

Deep Abdominal Breathing

This is the way we all breathed as babies, however as stress impacts our lives we begin to hold our breath more so we don't feel so much. The result is a life long habit of shallow breathing. Oxygen is key to our full health and energy levels, as it feeds our whole body. Please read the WARNING section before you try this exercise.

- Sit in a relaxed position or lie down
- Place one hand on your belly & the second on your chest.
- Breathe normally and be aware of which hand moves
- On next inhalation increase your inhale, feeling your rib cage expand more; notice if your belly also moves.
- Exhale gently and slowly
- Continue for at least 5 breathes
- Notice how you feel

WARNING: if you have been shallow breathing for years this extra oxygen rushing into your body can make you feel dizzy or light headed. If this occurs please return to regular breathing. If this does occur it is a sign that your body needs this exercise but you need to build up to it slowly just as you would when increasing your exercise levels.

WARNING: If you have **asthma** please bring your focus to your exhale more than your inhale. If you have any challenges with your breathing during this exercise please stop immediately.

Progressive Muscular Relaxation

This is a very simple technique that requires ten to fifteen minutes of practice once a day for you to start seeing results quickly. I love to practice this technique to relieve built up daily stress while I'm in bed; it also promotes better sleep at night.

I have also practiced this relaxation technique when my son was at his occupational therapy sessions. I would lie on the floor in the waiting room. Staff members were well used to me and I was always on my own. However I have also practiced it in many public places, even at the Guggenheim Museum in New York, the Natural History and Science Museums in San Diego.

I could be seen lying on a bench, eyes closed, ignoring the world around me. At this stage in my life I am beyond worrying about others looking at me and thinking I'm weird. I know I feel more relaxed than those others and my health and well-being means more to me than their opinions of me.

Progressive Muscular Relaxation is a deep muscle relaxation technique first discussed in a book by the same name by Doctor Edmund Jacobson, a Chicago physician in 1929. (Jacobson 1929) This technique helps to eliminate the built up tension in your muscles that occur as a natural response to the flight or fight response. When we have a lot of muscle tension in our bodies we are more prone to experiencing anxiety, counterbalancing this tension supports a calmer mind. It also has been found to be a great technique to apply to many ailments associated with stress such as depression, Irritable bowel syndrome, insomnia, fatigue, high blood pressure and muscle spasms.

Prior to my stress burnout I had chronic back pain. Once I started to practice **Progressive Muscular Relaxation** and regular **Yoga** this pain left and I no longer had to attend the chiropractor three times a week. It was a great relief to my bank account as well as my back.

Progressive relaxation allows you to become aware of what muscles you are chronically holding tension in. Often we don't even realize how tense a muscle is and what it feels for the same muscle to be in deep relaxation. I didn't until I started to practice this technique; now I have so much more muscle awareness which helps me to notice almost instantly when I am holding tension before it creates a bigger problem. This simple technique involves just tightening and consciously relaxing one muscle group at a time.

1. Allow yourself ten to fifteen minutes for this practice
2. To start find somewhere quiet to lye down where you feel your body is fully supported or if this is not possible you can sit in a comfortable chair where your neck is supported.
3. Close your eyes.
4. Clench your right hand tightly as you take a deep breathe in. Notice the tension in this muscle.
5. Let the hand relax on your exhalation. My favorite extra here is to say to at the same to myself "My hand is relaxing and letting go" or "My hand is melting and softening."
6. Repeat full sequence on right.
7. Notice how your right hand feels compared to your left hand.
8. Continue the same practice for the left hand.
9. Then clench both **fists** together.
10. Then bend the right **elbow** and tense your **bicep**.
11. Relax on your exhalation.
12. Repeat on left side. Notice how these muscles feel.
13. Bring awareness to your **face** and scrunch up the face, tightening forehead, cheeks, puckering your **lips** as if to kiss a mirror.
14. Then relax on the out breath – saying my face is softening and melting.
15. Repeat – Notice how your face feels.
16. If you have a longer period of time you can isolate the muscles groups on your face. For example just tighten the forehead, the follow with the eyes, then the lips, jaw etc.
17. Next focus on your **shoulders** scrunching them upwards towards your ears as you inhale.
18. Exhale relax and melt them.
19. Notice how they feel. Repeat.
20. Bring focus to head. Gentle push your head back onto the pillow beneath it. (Always be cautious with your **neck** as it is extra sensitive and easy to strain)
21. Roll gently side-to-side if it feels comfortable. Relax on exhale melting and softening.
22. Allow the body to deeply relax. Noticing how this feels.
23. You can continue this practice for the **buttocks, stomach, legs and feet**. Until the whole body is experiencing a deep muscular relaxation response.
24. ENJOY! Let us know how you got on our community Facebook page ☺.

Visualization or Guided Imagery

Visualization is a tool that everyone can use. You already practiced it in Chapter 6 when you remembered a success moment for yourself. You have used it all your life when you daydreamed or counted sheep to get to sleep. Below are two ways to apply it into your life to reduce everyday stress.

To understand visualization we must remember that there are different ways that we take in information – through the ears, eyes, body, nose and taste — auditory processing, visual and kinesthetic, scent and taste. When we remember something we access these different modalities associated with the memory. It may be the smell or texture that triggers the memory. Similarly when you are visualizing, you may find it easier to see a lot of visuals, while others are more aware of the textures, others the imagined smells.

So when creating your customized guided visualization, incorporate scents in the air, textures you can feel, scenery you can admire, colors you can feel expanded by. You are in control as this is all happening in your own imagination.

You can practice this quickly by closing your eyes and imagining you are eating your favorite fruit. See it, feel it, smell it, taste it – all in your mind. Notice does your mouth start to water? It usually does. Your brain doesn't know the difference between an imagined event and a real event if you have a full visceral experience while thinking about it.

There have been many studies done on the effectiveness of visualization as a tool for increasing well being and reducing stress.

The most recent study I researched was conducted in 2005 in Korea. Sixty women suffering from breast cancer were studied. Thirty patients were shown how to practice progressive muscle relaxation and guided visualization during their six months of chemotherapy. The other thirty patients were treated with just chemotherapy. (Pungnap-dong 2005)

The group that practiced the stress reducing tools experienced less nausea and vomiting, and had reduced anxiety and depression. Overall they felt more physically and emotionally balanced than those who received just chemotherapy alone. Six months after the trial ended the original group who had received the stress reduction training were still experiencing an overall better quality of life than the other group.

Many other studies have led to the same conclusion. The combination of Progressive Muscular Relaxation and Visualization can greatly improve quality of life through stress reduction and lessening symptoms associated with chronic stress.

Visualization for Pain Management

I have used this tool successfully to support myself when I had chronic back pain. First I would relax my body using some deep breathing techniques then allow myself to travel to the source of the pain in my body. I would ask myself what color this pain was and an image of the pain would appear in my inner knowing. Then I would focus on allowing the pain image to reduce and see it changing. Eventually the pain image would shrink or dissolve. Then I would fill the now empty pain space with a brighter and more energized color, what ever felt appropriate to bring healing to my body at that time.

I usually saw white or gold but sometimes turquoise and pink would appear too. My pain levels would be massively diminished. You can also ask the body while in a relaxed state: "What is causing the pain?" Be open to the answers that appear in your mind; they are always insightful and usually accurate. Personally I have found that although some of my back pain was caused by injury, these injuries were not extensive enough to cause the actual amount of chronic pain I was in. What was appearing in my body was a combination of some physical injury compounded by the avoidance of an emotionally painful situation, which I 'stuffed' into my back as opposed to dealing with it. I used to have a fear of crying, as I thought it was a weakness. Now I know that if I release my emotions in the moment or later in a safe environment that I am greatly supporting my overall well-being.

Guided Visualization for Stress Reduction

1. Begin by finding a comfortable place where you can be undisturbed. Close your eyes and use deep abdominal breathing to begin relaxing. If you are feeling very tense, then incorporate some progressive muscular relaxation before you begin trying to create a visualization for best results. Avoid drink caffeine before you begin as this impedes your ability to enter a deeper state of relaxation.

2. Create a safe place in your imagination for yourself to journey to.

3. Choose a place that is warm, comfortable, safe and nurturing, indoors or outside.

4. Begin to study all the details there—colors, shapes, sounds, textures, finding all these qualities within the surroundings your imagination has created for you.

5. Relax and rest. Feel your body relaxing, and feel happiness flow through your being.

6. If you have a particular question to ask, go ahead and ask it: What do I need to allow more of to feel more relaxed each day? How do I increase my health levels? What color would serve me right now? And so on.

7. You can spend as long here as you wish. (Five to thirty minutes)

8. When you are complete, thank this beautiful place for its relaxation and nurturing, and begin to allow yourself to come back to awareness of your current environment.

9. Notice any sounds you can hear around you. Notice what you can feel touching your skin. Notice how your body feels. Take a few deep breaths in. Stretch, yawn and slowly open your eyes, coming slowly and fully back into awareness of the present moment.

10. Write down any insights you received.

Yoga

Yoga is an ancient form of exercise, designed primarily to prepare the body for meditation by reducing stress and calming the monkey mind. When I first began practicing yoga over 20 years ago I hated it. My mind wouldn't calm down, my body was in such pain, and I felt constantly frustrated by my inability to do the poses in what I considered was a successful way. However after around five classes I began to feel less frustrated. My body was already feeling the benefit. My stress levels were too, and I was sleeping better on the days I took class. It was around this time that I decided to start a daily practice of just ten minutes a day. I did simple stretches to ease out my tight areas – shoulders, neck, hips, legs and back. I still do this today and benefit daily from this consist yet brief practice.

Yoga literally means union—of mind, body, and spirit. There are many forms of Yoga available— Hatha, Hot, Inyengar, Astanga, Bikram, Fitness, Kundalini, Gentle, Restorative, and Flow Yoga to name but a few styles available throughout the U.S. today. Even Naked Yoga has recently made quite a stir in some parts of the country, although I don't see myself taking that class anytime soon.

What type of Yoga Should I Practice?

- In brief, if you are new to yoga and living with a lot of stress then the restorative or gentle class will support you better for stress reduction.

- If you wish to use yoga as your primary form of exercise, then a class that has more standing poses and moves slightly faster such as a Hatha, or a flow class is probably more suited to your needs.

- If you are very fit and want an intense workout then Bikram, Astanga or fitness yoga is probably what you will be drawn too.

Although I usually practice a combination of yoga during my week to gain balance in the body. I have practiced Astanga, Kundalini, Hatha, Inyengar, restorative and gentle yoga during the last 20 years. I discovered that as my stress levels increased, from parenting, I needed to move slower and go deeper into the poses thus creating a deeper relaxation response in my body. This has been essential to maintaining my health levels. However all yoga is beneficial to the mind, body and spirit.

Summary:

There are many forms of techniques you can practice to support your efforts to reduce the buildup of negative stress in your body. The fact is that you have to actually take the responsibility to try some of these techniques and see which work best for you. Have fun with it; share the ideas with your family and friends. Even have a relaxation event at your home when your kids are at school. You will quickly feel the benefit, and wonder why you never tried them before. Let us know how you get on at our Facebook group.

Weekly Goal:

Between NOW and this date: ___/___/___, I choose to incorporate of a new Thrive Now Blueprint Stress Reducer.

_____
_____
_____
_____

Benefit to achieving this goal

_____
_____
_____
_____

Negative outcome if not achieved

_____
_____
_____
_____

How I feel after achieving this goal ☺

_____
_____
_____
_____

13

Wisdoms from the Front Line

"When we listen to people there is an alternating current, and this recharges us so that we never get tired of each other. We are constantly being re-created. There is this little creative fountain inside us that begins to spring and cast up new thoughts and unexpected laughter and wisdom."

Brenda Ueland **(1891-1985)**– American Journalist & Author

*A*s you read this chapter I invite you to listen with an open heart to other mothers' journeys. I did try to interview several fathers, but the dads I spoke to invited me to talk to their partners; they felt their partner did most of the front line work and could report and comment on the journey in a more comprehensive way. I know this finding is not specific to me. A recent study of parents of special needs children also found that the fathers felt the mothers had more knowledge to share in the study. In the end the study was rewritten to just focus on mothers and not "parents." (That article was titled "Parenting stress and psychological functioning among mothers of preschool children with autism and developmental delay" and appeared in Autism: International Journal of Research and Practice.) (Estes 2009)

The following transcripts are from mothers I interviewed. All have special needs children, ranging from those with Down Syndrome, Cerebral Palsy, and Autism to those who are Developmentally Delayed and Vision Impaired. In my efforts to bring a broad spectrum of views to you, I chose to go outside my own experience of parenting a child with autism so I could find what other wisdom and tools are being implemented by other moms on the front line, as I already mentioned more interview and wisdoms are available at www.ThriveNowToolKIT.com. I'm using the word front line to refer back to the beginning of the book where I quoted research that showed that mom's with autistic children had similar stress chemicals in their blood work to that of soldiers in battle.

It has been my awareness that often we judge others for having an easier life, more money, more resources, less disabilities to deal with etc. when in truth we are all dealing with challenges regardless of what "special need" our children have. I hope you enjoy these wisdoms and find them inspirational and enriching.

Jannirose JOY is our first special needs mom highlighted in our *'Wisdoms from the Front Line'*. She talks about her need to look deeply at herself with as much awareness as possible.

Jannirose JOY

Over 19 years ago, Jannirose JOY and her husband, a colonel in the US air force, made the decision to adopt a child with Down Syndrome whom they called Charlie. Charlie has blossomed into a magical, loving, beautiful soul. He is a love ambassador who has read his poetry at many memorial services, weddings and other special occasions. Charlie's gift is to open hearts, and he changes people's lives with his unconditional love and enthusiasm for life. Like his mother, who is a Minister of Spiritual Peacemaking, Charlie was ordained in August 2012 by best-selling author and Peace Troubadour, James Twyman. Jannirose is a speaker and transformational teacher; she is the author of the upcoming book
Loving Outside the Lines: Lessons from an Earth Angel.

Jannirose shared:

"I figured out a long time ago that the most important piece of creating harmony in my family was to look at myself deeply with as much of my awareness as possible. That is what I have really focused on to help myself be the best parent that I can be and I am still learning each day.... Just learning how to let go of things, how to find peace in me, how to be more calm as a parent and not so reactive. In all families you have such a different mix of people all together in the same space. There are always going to be lots of 'invitations' to learn how to work together and create harmony together. Invitation to me is such a friendly word compared to what most of us think as moments of frustrations.

It is about shifting perspective. It was a CHOICE that I made for myself so that I could have a nicer life because I wasn't always this way. I learned a lot of negative ways growing up but they weren't working for me, it was not fun. It was not fun to be that version of me. I didn't know how to cope and I held onto things forever. It felt really horrible so I had to make a choice. Interestingly I can still fall into that place but now I know how to get out of it quickly."

Visit Jannirose Joy's website to find out more about her and the magical words create by Earth Angel - Charlie Fenimore at www.JanniroseJoy.com

Sarah Wycoff

Sarah is the founder of the Free Heart Ranch where she runs retreats for parents of special needs children. Sarah holds a master's degree in physical education, psychology and dance movement therapy. She is certified in feminine power as a transformational coach. The mom of a very special boy, Zion, who is legally blind and developmentally delayed, at one point she was told that Zion may never walk or talk. Sarah was widowed when Zion was only a baby, which left her in a place of great uncertainty and financial struggle. Now Zion is eighteen and both Sarah and he are thriving. She found that connecting deeply with her intuitive feminine self and choosing to look deeply and to nurture herself were the greatest gift she could bring to herself and her son.

Sarah shared how parenting Zion has changed her life:

"I had this period of time that I look back on it now and I was really in shock. This had a lot to do with that series of events that just kept taking me farther and farther out of where I had expected to be going. I just didn't have the where-with-all or the resources, or it wasn't the right timing, or whatever, for me to actually be able to land with my feet on the ground and be in an empowered place.

So one of the reasons I now have the relationship with my son that I do, is that after that period of time of just being in shock, it was clear to me that

Zion really was, still is, an avenue for my greatest awakening because it was the place of my greatest discomfort. Discomfort doesn't even describe it. I was in excruciating pain just at the thought of being alone and being the parent of a child that I didn't understand and who had so many difficulties, etc., etc. So shamelessly, I used him for my own personal growth.

Not long after my husband's death I visited an adoption shelter just to talk of the possibility of having another family bring Zion into their family. It didn't take me long to realize that I could never, ever, ever, let somebody else make life decisions for him. I wanted to be the one to love him. I knew that as imperfect as I was, I was perfect for him. I really made the choice. It didn't make it any easier right then and there. There was so much learning I had to do; I actually let myself decide freely to step into it.

I didn't think of it as wise at the time, but I look back on that willingness to visit that adoption counselor as a wise thing. I felt not exactly ashamed about it for a while, but certainly not proud of it. It's not something that I'm proud of now even. I had to actually take some steps to re-choose, actually many times, but at this time in a very significant way, re-choose to be Zion's solo parent; Zion's mom. And to make that choice with full willingness.

Some years after I really made that conscious choice, probably when my son was around two years old, I had a light bulb moment. I reached a deep understanding that there is no separation between loving, caring for, being in service of, and being responsible to Zion. There is no separation between any of that and my doing all of those exact things for myself. I really deeply understood that everything that I needed and desired in the world served him that I would be at my best availability to love him if I was loving myself the best I possibly could, whatever that meant.

Another key piece for me to understand was that when I was faced with a choice between doing something that would really nourish me and doing something for him, I would ask myself, "Okay, do I really need this?"

If yes was the response, then even if it looked, in the immediate moment, like I was depriving him of something, I actually was not, for there is no separation here. That was a big piece for me to understand. I had gotten to that point because I had become fairly depleted and was not able to love him the way I really wanted to. I really needed to recognize that I needed to have fun. I needed to have a lover. I needed to exercise my friendship and my creativity and more. So little by little I stepped more fully into life"

When I asked about her work and how she helps herself and others:
"I have been bringing together an understanding that the hyper-masculinized ways of creating in life that we've been educated in and acculturated to for hundreds of thousands of years has gotten us to a wonderful place, but it's also gotten us into this kind of stuck place individually and collectively.

So being able to bring forward things like intuition, uncertainty, the ability to be related and to work together for solutions in a way that's very generative of a solution for a future that we want to live in, that's really what I'm interested in helping people to step more into. There are some very specific tools and practices that can get us there and these blend beautifully with the movement therapy and the expressive art that I facilitate because bringing forward some of the feminine characteristics in anybody, whether it's a man or a woman, it's a process. It's a personal process.

It's a process oriented towards developing a willingness to not have to control where the process goes. We have a vision of the endpoint and we're going to make it look this way or else. That's kind of what we've been taught to respect the most. So being able to just engage in the process of oriented creative experience, not only is so refreshing, it results in something that's deeply meaningful. It actually comes from whether you call it psyche or the deeper self. It can continue to inform and speak to the artist within. I really feel like we're all artists in that way."

I still move through that sometimes as a parent and a person, of pressuring myself to do something because I'm either perceiving or have been informed that somebody else or some entity has an expectation of me doing something a particular way. It feels terrible, especially when it doesn't match what authentically wants to be created through me.

So, wow, when we put that on our children... Let me put it this way. When we remove that pressure as a parent from our children, it is such a blessing to all concerned.

Having super sensitive children really is a beautiful and meaningful aspect of life. But what an opportunity to sort of be, certainly not forced, but very deeply encouraged into a new way of functioning because our children are functioning in such a different way that it calls the newness from us.

So being willing to turn more toward intuition, in my own experience and in working with others, I just call it making a friend with uncertainty. Being able to see uncertainty as a partner in what it is that I would like to create in my life and being happy for my son, and really have this allowing instead of acting like an enemy. Like you said earlier, I think before the recording, just actually being in a state of allowing our creativity to generate the future we would like."

Visit Sarah Wyckoff's website to find out more about her and the powerful work she facilitates with art therapy, retreats and transformational coaching www.FreeHeartRanch.com

Nancy Battye

Nancy is a coach, author, inspirational teacher and single mom with three children, twin girls with cerebral palsy and a son who is without disability. To contact Nancy visit www.NancyBattye.com. Nancy offers tele-seminars on compassion and self-love, hosts a radio show, and is in the process of developing a foundation for parents of special needs children so families can have supported vacations with their disabled children. Nancy inspires me. In my words she has made 'diamonds out of coal'.

Nancy's marriage dissolved shortly after the birth of her twins, leaving her in a position of total caregiver for three children, two with severe health issues that required constant emergency medical intervention. She was penniless, isolated, exhausted and beyond overwhelm, yet today, she thrives.

During my interview with Nancy she spoke about literally living on survival mode, in a state of complete unawareness as to how she was creating disease for herself. She was trying to be perfect, overworking herself as a constant caregiver without a partner, support or any extended family. Her lessons at the time were hard, and self-care was an unconsidered luxury. Yet now that she has recovered from severe health challenges that were created from her lack of self-care, she fully recognizes her mistakes.

Years later, on reflection, she realized that her perfectionism and messages she had taken on as a child from her family and community had not allowed her to ask for help, or to even consider the need for help. She believed she 'should' be able to do it ALL, from raising her children, caring for them 24/7, to fixing the plumbing, to being the sole provider, to repairing the car, whatever it took. Nancy never stopped to consider the toll her perfectionism was taking on her life until she was faced with the hardest decision a mother should never have to make.

"No help. I know for myself, that was one of the most difficult experiences in my life. By the time my girls were 10, I was so physically depleted from having done everything on my own for 10 years; four hours of sleep interrupted. Not four continuous hours, but four hours of interrupted sleep every night for 10 years. Some nights no sleep at all depending on whether we were in the hospital and different things going on, so physically depleted. I got to the place where I couldn't lift up a piece of paper. I couldn't lift up the car keys. I was putting milk in the cupboard where the cleaners went and I was putting cleaner in the fridge where the milk was supposed to go and I wasn't even realizing I was doing it. Then the next time I'd open the fridge I'd be like, "I wonder what that is and I wonder why it's there. I wonder what happened to the milk." And I started dropping things. At first I thought, "Oh, I'm just not paying enough attention." I'd try it again; I'd drop things again.

It became very serious, very quickly. I blew out my knee, my ACL that is the stability in our knees for our core and our body strength. I went through the most painful thing in my life. Everything I went through with delivering my girls was nothing compared to the pain when I blew out my knee. I went to a specialist. He looked at me and said, "Oh, you need to have surgery. And you can't do any lifting for four months."

"You're out of your mind", I said. "Don't you know anything about my life whatsoever?"

I carried on trying to survive without surgery so my children could be served, and then one day I was carrying my daughter, Tina, in my arms, and I slipped. My leg gave out. I fell backwards and cradled her to protector her. This was a defining moment for me.

The realization that, holy cow, this is serious. If something happens to me and I end up in the hospital incapacitated, what's going to happen to them? That scared the living daylights out of me.

So I had to make the decision to put my kids into foster care, which was the most horrendous decision of my life. It created such guilt and shame at having to put my kids into care.

We are very powerful people. Fear can be very levitating and also so powerful. It's so easy to get into a situation and get lost so quickly without realizing it, after having done an amazing job for so many years.
Yet, what I recognize and have understood and discovered about myself is the level of self-care, the degree to which I could have had a much greater

sense of self-care was not there because so much of what I did to deal in the moment with what I needed to deal with came from a lot of guilt or just expectation from the perspective of growing up. It's like, well, Nancy, you are defined by who you are in terms of how hard you work. If you're constantly striving and working for perfection, at some point in time, you will reach a level of perfection. And then at that point in time, somebody will grant you his or her love and acceptance. I was driven from a need to just be perfect. Asking for help was a sign of weakness. Life must be a test. Man, I got to pass.

As parents of special needs children we can get so caught up in, "No, this is what my child needs. This is what I need to do. Then this is what my other child that doesn't have any disabilities needs. And this is what my spouse needs. And this is what others around me need. " What about what we need? That goes by the wayside. And before we realize it, so much time has passed by.

Well, what I didn't realize until the most recent years is that love and acceptance that I had been searching for was really something that was about myself that really only comes from myself. I didn't know at the time that I didn't have full love and acceptance. I didn't know that my driving needs were being met by or being fueled, rather, by my need to get to a level of acceptance…

We can all find some space to have some self-care… Even if it's simply standing and looking at ourselves in the mirror when brushing our teeth, smiling, looking in to those beautiful eyes of ours and saying, "You know what, I love you. I respect you. Do you know how proud I am of you and the job that you're doing?"

What a beautiful gift we offer to our children for us to model that for them. When we're able to open up that space for ourselves, I so firmly believe that it allows us a much greater capacity to give that compassion and offer that compassion to other people in the world. So from there, we lessen judgment. We know we close the gaps, right, where there are no more bridges to walk across. We're not judging so harshly. We're more concerned. We're more loving. It all starts with us…"

> **If you feel you have wisdoms to share with other parents of special needs children I would love to hear from you please email me your stories to Stories@ThriveNowBlueprint.com and or share them on our facebook community page**

14

Spirituality: A Faster Path to Peace

"Happiness cannot be traveled to, owned, earned, worn or consumed. Happiness is the spiritual experience of living every minute with love, grace and gratitude."
Denis E Waitley (1933 – present) Motivational Speaker & Author

Spirituality – oh, if only I had the time, the space, the money and the babysitter! Isn't spirituality for those who can afford the time for it? For those with kids who will wear the buttoned down shirts and sit dutifully in church on a Sunday morning! Not us – right?

Yet as I maneuver my way through this life of parenting often-challenging children, I believe that self-awareness, stress management tools, a deeper connection to my own inner voice and to that of a higher wisdom have kept me sane. Seeing the world as sacred and having gratitude for small blessings keeps me thriving. Somehow getting kicked in the shins by your own child doesn't seem so bad when you have a deeper sense of inner peace!

Spirituality isn't about having blind faith or misguided notions of the world being perfect and ideal. I live in a VERY REAL WORLD! Often under duress and experiencing extreme conditions, I have no family support as they all live abroad. I don't always get it right as a parent and I don't always stay as calm as I would like to. But to this date I haven't stabbed anyone with a pencil and, as I am an exceptionally hotheaded Viking from Ireland, this can seem a miracle to those who've heard the total rubbish our family has had to put up with year after year, within the systems that are supposedly there to support our children. My friends all tell me I am the most patient person they have ever met; yet I wasn't born with patience. My mom will tell you I behaved like a real redhead.

However, years ago, when I burnt out from stress, I literally had to recreate my internal view point of the world in order to recover my well being.

I discovered that true happiness comes from an internal experience not an external one. Self-trust and self-love are probably the two most important contributors to discovering inner peace and not feeling murderous towards those who are thwarting your best efforts at IEP meetings (Individual Education Plans) or overwhelming on the floor as you are trying to go out for your first date night in months!

There have been many occasions when I could feel my blood begin to boil while sitting in meetings, yet every time I have been able to take a deep breath and send love firstly to myself, then to all those sitting around the table, knowing that whatever the outcome everything would be "perfect" as a bigger plan was in place.

Even when the school district lost my son's paperwork *twice* and he completely fell through the cracks, even when they lost the letter I wrote requesting support and they ignored multiple phone calls while we were in crisis, even when my son was misdiagnosed, there was always a silver lining waiting to reveal itself down the road— though of course we were not aware of it at the time. And if I hadn't been reduced to a state of such exhaustion in my twenties, I would never have had the tools I now use daily to support myself in such situations.

So what seemed as a total disaster at the age of twenty-four turned out to be the greatest gift at age forty-four. I have discovered that life always sends solutions if you are open to receiving them, just as you are now reading this book and empowering yourself to create a different experience for yourself on a daily basis.

Allowing ourselves to trust our inner wisdom or intuition requires us to be in a place of connection and relaxation, not fear and separation. This deeper sense of inner peace has strongly supported me in parenting my beloved sons. Over the last twelve years, there have been many times when I recognize I could have been sent over the edge and triggered into a major meltdown. But having this sense of internal calm has supported me so I can stay more present to observe my reactions and in turn support myself in making clearer choices. Of course I am human so I am constantly in a place of practice and not perfection, constantly striving to make better choices and add more conscious moments into my day. Sometimes I get it right and other times my own emotional triggers interrupt even my most Zen moments; however, my recovery time is usually fast. My awareness turns inward and I notice what created the trigger. Kicking my negative internal critic to the curb has become easier and easier with practice.

My two sons have attended a total of eight different schools in the most recent years. This has been due mostly to my eldest son's behavior challenges that required us to move him to different schools, so we could find specialized campuses to support him. Within each new school we had to create systems that would work to assist our sons.

One school principal deliberately worked against us, sabotaging two IEP meetings, creating drama, denying that our youngest son had any special needs at the IEP— even after the experts had shown that he indeed had significant challenges that needed understanding and support. He did not have autism; rather his auditory and visual processing issues greatly affected his ability to learn in a large noisy classroom. The school authorities also openly discussed our case at a public meeting and made intimidating remarks to my husband. At the same time this was occurring, my husband was out of work.

So our family was under much more stress than usual. This was not the first extremely challenging time we had undergone as a family. Just having a child on the autism spectrum, plus a second that needs extra support, is challenging enough. But add to that little or no community support and an extended family that lives abroad and you could have a recipe for disaster.

This is why I say that my stress burn out was the best thing that has ever happened to me; if I hadn't discovered so many tools and strategies to heal and support myself then, I'm sure I would have gone over the edge. Yet my many tools—such as those described in the previous chapters— and my sense of deep inner peace have created a powerful combination that allows me to stay more balanced.

We have already spoken at length about how to create the relaxation aspect of self-care. Now I want to expand on how to create the deeper spiritual connection that fosters self-trust and makes listening to your own inner wisdom much easier. This inner wisdom is what makes mothers take action when they know their child is very sick, yet others are telling them there is nothing to worry about.

This is the intuition that I have been consciously working with and building upon for more than twenty years, and that has allowed me to guide clients from all over the world with my deep spiritual gifts as well as supporting them with practical stress management strategies.

To me, spirituality means connection: connection to myself, connection to my purpose, connection to the energy of the life force, connection to those around me, connection to God.

Spirituality to me is not about religion, it is not about any one doctrine or faith; however, having a strong spiritual connection enhances whatever doctrine or faith you are drawn too.

For me, connection is the essence of life, that divine spark that lives within each one of us. It can be a unifying aspect for humanity. I use the word God here as an anchor point, however I do not mean God in relationship to any one religion. I use the concept of the Divine to express life-force energy and unconditional love energy.

That energy, I believe, is an aspect of everything in our world, it is an energy that we can access and allow to flow through us, and the amount of this energy that we allow to flow through us greatly impacts our vitality levels, our *joie de vivre*, our ability to develop full self-awareness and our ability to find lasting inner peace.

We have a choice to allow or disallow this energy. Spirituality connects us to that God-force energy, and it doesn't have any one path. Multiple paths can take us to that sense of connection, and no one belief or person is right or wrong.

Often we hear there is one way to become enlightened: "Follow me over here because I have the only answer." My experience has shown that just as each of us is completely unique, so is our spiritual pathway to inner peace.

I believe that we are made in the likeness of God, that we are a spark of God's energy on earth, God in action, God in motion. Our greatest challenge is how to live from a place that allows us to be the fullest expression of our truth and beauty in the world, while managing our day-to-day lives in a highly stressful environment. Parenting our special kids can require us to be in a constant state of caring for others and in doing so we can lose ourselves and become disconnected from our own purpose and passion.

I often ask my clients:

"If you were God how would you treat yourself?"

I don't mean that in an egotistical way, I mean if you are truly made in the likeness of God and you truly love yourself because you are enough just as you are, then how might you treat yourself differently from the way you are treating yourself today?

Take a moment to close your eyes and consider this: How would you treat yourself if you were the most important person in the world? To your child you already are!

_____

_____

_____

_____

_____

Were you surprised in any way by what was revealed to you in the last exercise? Often we are! When I recently invited a room full of special parents and service providers to consider this very question, I saw tears glistening in many eyes. Later the group shared that they only realized in that moment just how much they had been impeding their health and wellness by putting everyone's needs before their own.

So I urge you to take note of your inner voice. I urge you to take action on what was revealed to you on how to nurture yourself more. I honor you for taking the time to truly know that you are important.

We have already spoken about our self-talk and how much of it can be negative. Honestly, if we spoke to others the way we usually speak to ourselves then we would be very lonely in the world.

This "I'm not good enough" conversation comes from our low self-esteem and our upbringing. But it also comes from a deep feeling of being separate from God. Our fears and anxieties as well as our wars are all created from a viewpoint that there is not enough and we are not enough. Wars are never started because everyone involved feels they are the same, or that those they are fighting are equal to them. They always come from a place of greed, separation and fear!

> **"We are not human beings having a spiritual experience. We are spiritual beings having a human experience."**
> Pierre Teilhard de Chardin (1881 – 1955)– French Philosopher

For me I find great connection in yoga, dancing, a daily gratitude practice, mindfulness meditation, being in nature, being beside the sea, eating organic raw food, chanting and singing, hugging my boys, laughing with friends, being intimate with my husband: all of these activities increase my ability to feel more connected to God-force energy. And that is a unique experience for each individual.

What experiences make you feel more peaceful and alive?

_____
_____
_____
_____
_____

When I was a child I had a great teacher. Her name was Sister Regina, a Catholic nun. She taught me to see the beauty in everything, to study nature deeply and see God in ALL, to marvel at the small things in life that others took for granted.

I was only eight when I entered her class, but her teachings still impact me today. She gave me a different perspective on life, showing me that life wasn't all about getting A's or having stuff. There was something bigger and much grander afoot in our world. She emanated joy, and to this day, she has been one of the happiest people I have ever met. She was always singing and had the calm energy of peace and contentment that still stands out in my memory.

For many years I thought I would become a nun because I was so inspired by this woman. And, as I noted before, I discovered boys and that idea flew out the window. Nonetheless, she instilled in me a sense of curiosity to think differently, to follow my heart and inner wisdom.

I think we often feel challenged because we look outside ourselves instead of listening to our own internal wisdom. However, as parents of special needs children, we do not have the luxury of spending long periods of time in retreat to find inner peace, as was the way of our spiritual teachers of the past such as our beloved Jesus, who spent forty days and forty nights in the desert to reach a deeper connection to God. For us such a retreat is just not an option.

For our family even going to church can be a challenge as my eldest son can be disruptive — running, making noise or overwhelming in the crowd. So I needed to find a way that worked for me, not a way that **created guilt** for what **I wasn't able to do** or how I wasn't able to show up. And this is what I encourage you to do.

If you find yourself in a place of guilt or shame or in that "I'm not good enough" internal conversation, then you know you are moving away from your spiritual path. If you find yourself in a place of laughter, love, excitement and deep contentment then you are on or moving closer to your spiritual path. **Our feelings are the best compass we have as our guide**.

One theme I have seen over and over again from spending so many years working with women is that it is not okay for us to take time for ourselves without feelings of guilt. Often we feel we have to qualify every decision involving making space just for ourselves. In the same way as when someone admires your new top and you hear yourself say, "Oh I got it on sale", we do the same with creating space for self-care and a deeper spiritual life. We hide it. We hide it and create guilt usually because, within our family of origin, this was not an acceptable thing. For me, the martyr syndrome was hard to break, as it had been so en-grained into me as part of my upbringing and cultural background. I was always hearing myself over-explain whatever was for me. I could only go for a massage, for example, if I was in pain, not because it would give me pleasure and nurture my body.

Are there areas in your own life in which you find yourself making similar excuses?

_____

_____

_____

_____

_____

The spiritual path does not have to be strived towards. The small things in life create the path ahead. Just to be as a child deep in play and flow while experiencing pure joy: this to me is a spiritual path. Yet the child didn't need to be taught this; it is just his or her natural state. However, as we get older and take on the attitudes of those around us, including anxiety, stress and fear, we forget the natural flow we once had when we found ourselves in that playtime as a child. This is where we flow; this is were we light up.

Can you remember that childhood flow energy for yourself? What was it like?

_____
_____
_____
_____
_____
_____
_____

What were your favorite games to play? Doing what gave you the most fun?

_____
_____
_____
_____
_____
_____
_____

Here are some of my favorite childhood games:
- I ran a clinic for injured bugs in my garage – playing the healer and nurse.
- I was always mothering my dollies.
- Everything I learnt at school I would come home and teach to my dollies and teddies using my chalkboard to create my own classroom.

And to this day I am happiest when I am offering healing support to my clients, speaking and teaching and spending time with my boys. It is in these pursuits that I feel most myself—most aligned, most in flow and most at peace. WHAT IS TRUE FOR YOU? Where do you feel most alive, what creates passion for you? If you have forgotten, reflect on this exercise and see how you can begin to incorporate some of the energy that excited you as a child back into your life? Or, if you already are working with some of it, how can you enhance it? Incorporating some of this youthful, innocent energy into your life again gives you another avenue to inner peace through passion building.

Conclusion

As you will see there are many ways to manage your stress levels and support yourself while parenting your special child or adult. I have taught groups from senior executives to gypsies these same techniques and all received benefit from them.

Deciding which ones work best for you and your busy schedule is the key to success. The majority of the strategies I have given you can be practiced for ten minutes a day and you will receive increased relaxation as a result. Using time in bed works well for me too. This is where I practice progressive muscular relaxation, visualization, gentle yoga stretches and deep abdominal breathing. However, you don't have to wait for bedtime to reduce the stress on your body. Remember! Little relaxations prevent stress from building up and increase your energy levels throughout your day. Finding a way to create more joy and passion-filled living is a wonderful support for your stress reduction. Creating space to develop deeper self-awareness, as well as listening to your own inner knowing, for in truth, as the great revolutionary thinker Albert Einstein told us:

"No problem can be solved from the same level of consciousness that created it"

Albert Einstein (1879 –1955)
Nobel Prize Winner & Theoretical Physicist

Shifting your consciousness—a process that reading and engaging in this book will have begun to create—is the path to all healing. It is also the pathway to creating more harmony in your family life. When parents begin to create a deeper sense of peace, the positive impact that occurs within the family is unmistakable. Personally this is still my favorite "side effect" of looking after myself.

Allow me to repeat this main point: **Nurturing Yourself** may sometimes feel like a totally selfish act; however, it is in fact the most selfless act you can involve yourself in as the benefits move far beyond just your own health, well-being and more energized life. All around you bask in the glow of your feel good energy too. Have fun with these tools and exercises, and please share your "aha" moments and any requests for support at our Facebook group at www.facebook.com/ThriveNowBlueprint

To further support this learning and new lifestyle, I will be offering a series of online programs for you to continue and build on the work you began within this book. You are not alone on this journey. Support, community and practical advice will be available for you.

VISIT www.SiobhanWilcox.com to find out more about upcoming programs and other resources I have available. Also know that a percentage of all profits from my books and programs is given to various non-profits that support families living with special needs children. I am excited to be able to service and support those that make a difference in our lives everyday. I look forward to connect with you and supporting you soon.

Weekly Goal:

Between NOW and this date: ___/___/___, I choose to create a deeper spiritual practice by.....

_____
_____
_____
_____

Benefit to achieving this goal

_____
_____
_____
_____

Negative outcome if not achieved

_____
_____
_____
_____

How I feel after achieving this goal ☺

_____
_____
_____
_____

Recommended Reading

You Can Heal Your Life by Louise L Hay

The Power of Intention by Dr. Wayne W. Dyer.

The Power of Now: A Guide to Spiritual Enlightenment by Eckhart Tolle

Spontaneous Healing: How to Discover and Embrace Your Body's Natural Ability to Maintain and Heal Itself by Dr. Andrew Weil MD

The Seven Spiritual Laws of Success: A Practical Guide to the Fulfillment of Your Dreams by Deepak Chopra

The Relaxation and Stress Reduction Workbook by Martha Davis, Elizabeth Robbins Eshelman and Matthew McKay

The Anxiety and Phobia Workbook by Edmund J. Bourne

The Tapping Solution: A Revolutionary System for Stress-Free Living by Nick Ortner

Tapping Into Ultimate Success: How to Overcome Any Obstacle and Skyrocket Your Results by Jack Canfield and Pamela Bruner

Bibliography

Bradshaw, John. *Homecoming: Reclaiming and Championing Your Inner Child.* 1992.

Code, David. *Kids Pick Up on Everything: HOw Parental Stress is Toxic to Kids.* 2011.

Cohen, Sheldon. "How Stress Influences Disease." *Carnegie Mellon University.* 2012.

Doctor Raj Raghunathan, Ph.D,. "How Negative is Your 'Mental Chatter'." *Psychology Today*, Oct 2013.

Dodge, Dr Norman. *The Brain that Changes Itself.* Penguin, 2007.

Estes, Annette. "Parenting stress and psychological functioning among mothers of preschool children with autism and developmental delay." *Autism: International Journal of Research and Practice*, 2009.

Fritz Hollwich, B Dieckhues. "The Effect of Natural and Artificial Light Via the Eye on the Hormonal and Metabolic Balance of Animal and Man." *Opthalmologica vol. 180, no 4*, 1980: 188-197.

Jacobson, Doctor Edmund. *Progressive Muscular Relaxation.* 1929.

Lama, Dalai. *Path to Tranquility: Daily Wisdom.* Penguin, 1998.

Marmot, Professor Sir Michael. "Whitehall II (also known as the Stress & Health Study)." 2007.

Marsha Mailick Seltzer, Leann E. Smith, Jinkuk Hong, Jan S. Greenberg, David M. Almeida, Somer L. Bishop. "ORIGINAL PAPER Daily Experiences Among Mothers of Adolescents and Adults with Autism Spectrum Disorder." University of Wisconsin-Madison, 2009.

Martha Davis, PH.D. Elizabeth Robbins Eshelman M.S.W, & Matthew McKay PH.D. *The Relaxation & Stress Reduction Workbook.* 2007.

Medicine, David Mandell - Penn. "Impact that Autism has on Family Income." Center for Autism Research at the Children's Hospital of Philadelphia and associate director of the Center for Mental Health Policy and Services Research at the University of Pennsylvania, March 2012.

Pungnap-dong, Songpa-gu. "Efficacy of progressive muscle relaxation training and guided imagery in reducing chemotherapy side effects in patients with breast cancer and in improving their quality of life." *Department of Psychiatry, Asan Medical Center, University of Ulsan College of Medicine*, Oct 2005: 826-33.

Singh, Nirbhay N. ""Mindful Staff Can Reduce the Use of Physical Restraints When Providing Care to Individuals with Intellectual Disabilities."" *The Journal of Applied Research in Intellectual Disabilities*, 2009.

Weikle, Julia E. "Self-Talk & Self-Health." 1993.

What the Bleep Do We Know? - Down The Rabbit Hole. 2006.

About the Author

"My goal is simple: I love to inspire, support and create transformation for those who work with me. It is my mission to positively impact the lives of one million people by the end of 2015- allowing them to THRIVE NOW!"

Originally from Dublin, Ireland **Siobhan Wilcox** now lives in Encinitas, California. She is the mother of two beautiful boys, one on the autism spectrum, and is married to Paul John Ward, a business consultant and creator of Reconnective Coaching & Consultancy. Her children have been her greatest teachers to date.

Siobhan has studied many different areas related to increasing wellbeing and health since 1990 with now have over 3,000 hours of training in the areas of Training and Education, Counseling Skills, Stress Management, Yoga, Meditation, Mindfulness and Holistic Therapies.

She created SMPG (Stress Management & Personal Growth) Training & Consultancy in 1998, offering customized workshops for large corporations and government-run community projects in Ireland. This was a very successful business with many clients being supported by her. During this period she facilitated learning for many levels of staff from senior managers to administration. Siobhan also worked with various government-funded project and charities creating training for many wonderful groups such as the long-term unemployed, single parents from low-income backgrounds, Gypsies and recovering drug addicts.

This work also lead her to be interviewed on national TV and radio as an expert in the areas of increasing healing, self-care & sensitive children as well as being interviewed for magazine and newspaper articles.

With an office in Encinitas, Siobhan spends her days supporting her clients via Skype around the world, speaking, training, playing with her kids and going to the beach to meditate.

Email Siobhan at Siobhan@SiobhanWilcox.com to book her for media appearances, speaking or training opportunities. To book Siobhan for Coaching Sessions email Sessions@SiobhanWilcox.com

If you would like special needs children and their families to continue to Thrive, I ask that you volunteer for or financially support nonprofit organizations in your community. I've listed my favorite non-profits on my website www.ThriveNowBlueprint.com, each of whom is making a dramatic difference in your world by serving special children, their families and our communities. To this date a portion of all proceeds from the Thrive Now Blueprint book and programs has been donated to these organizations. You can learn more about these organizations on their respective websites.

Made in the USA
San Bernardino, CA
15 November 2014